In Celebration of
an Everyday Favourite

LITTLE GEM

APPLE

OVER 80 RECIPES INSPIRED
BY THE FINEST OF BRITISH FRUIT

J. BLISSITT

Jacqui Blissitt

CP

Caulton Press

FOR MUM

Love Always

For more apple-inspired recipes and for information
about suppliers please go to:

littlegemapple.co.uk

First published by Caulton Press Ltd in 2018

www.caultonpress.co.uk

1 3 5 7 9 10 8 6 4 2

Copyright © Caulton Press Ltd

J. Blissitt asserts her moral rights
as the author of this work.

Cover illustrations: 'Yorkshire Beauty' (front cover, left),
'Loddington' (front cover, right) and 'Cox's Orange Pippin'
(back cover) from *The Herefordshire Pomona – facsimile* CD ROM,
2005. Reproduced by kind permission of Marcher Apple Network.

Text and photographs © Caulton Press Ltd

ISBN 978-1-9164759-0-8

Printed and bound in Slovenia

Contents

INTRODUCTION

The idea for this book came from a visit to my parents' house. Whilst taking the customary turn around the garden to inspect the latest goings-on I regarded the apple tree – a Howgate Wonder – so familiar from my childhood. Now slightly gnarled with age, it was absolutely laden with large, red-streaked green fruit – the old-fashioned kind depicted in storybooks. Too many to eat the rest were simply left for the garden birds, which struck me as rather a pity. Not for the birds, of course, but a shame nonetheless. To pass the time on the journey home I started compiling a mental list of all the different uses for this remarkable but often overlooked, everyday fruit. Thus the seed of this cookbook was sown.

Growing up in the New Forest I perhaps took apples for granted. The frequent afterschool refrain of 'I'm hungry' was almost always met with the suggestion of an apple, fresh from the tree at certain times of year. Yet to my shame, I usually opted for a biscuit instead.

It is fair to say that the book in front of you today is very different to the one I originally had in mind. The plan was always to write a book of recipes – let the apples speak for themselves, I thought – however as I started my research time and again I found myself reading about the decline of traditional British orchards and the resulting and tragic loss of so many of our heritage varieties. It therefore became impossible to write this book without it ultimately being a call to action; an entreaty to celebrate what we have; a cautionary tale of how deeper this loss will penetrate if we don't. Perhaps in the end this is penance for those biscuits.

First and foremost I have tried to show the breadth of uses for this most versatile of fruits: from traditional British recipes such as Shropshire Fidget Pie and West Country Apple Dappy, to less familiar favourites from around the world such as Peruvian Crazy Water and Ozark Pudding, to updates on classics such as Blackberry & Apple Crumble Slice, because, try as I might, nothing would ever compare to my mum's homemade apple crumble.

.   .   .

The British have long had a love affair with the apple. In 2016 we consumed 625,000 tonnes[1] of culinary and dessert apples and despite competition from such johnny-come-latelies as the grape and banana, the apple remains one of the UK's best-loved fruits.

British apples are renowned for their exceptional taste and flavour. The quality of home-grown apples is largely due to the Great British weather. A mild climate allows the fruit to grow relatively slowly, leaving time for the flavour to fully develop. Regular rainfall produces good levels of juice, whilst the lack of extreme temperature fluctuations gives rise to a crisp texture. Of course flavour and texture shift according to variety, but it is this rich diversity that makes British apples so special.

With around 6,000 cultivars (cultivated varieties) documented to have been growing in the UK between 1853 and 1968[2], Britain once produced the highest number of apple varieties in the world. However a sharp increase in cheap, imported varieties such as Golden Delicious and Granny Smith, and the over-reliance by retailers on a just handful of dependable but dull domestic varieties, has led to a marked and serious decline in UK production.

In the last fifty years or so, two-thirds of the nation's orchards have been lost – grubbed up and replanted with cereal crops or used for housing development. Of the 2,000 varieties grown in the UK, only a dozen or so are widely known today. Many hundreds of old varieties, particular to different parts of the country, such as Kitchen Door from Maidstone, Lady Thornycroft from Bembridge on the Isle of Wight and Martin's Custard from the Leicestershire/Northamptonshire border have simply disappeared.

With each new loss, we erase not only our cultural heritage, but potentially valuable genetic resources.

There is, however, some good news emerging from recent DNA profiling. A national 'fruit fingerprinting' scheme, administered by Peter Laws of FruitID.com with DNA analysis provided by East Malling Research in Kent, has resolved some of the confusion around synonymy and distinctiveness. Some of the fruit sent in have been known varieties, but with a local name, some are unique to different places and a few interesting, sometimes unnamed samples have come to light for the first time.

Furthermore steps are now being taken to protect the diversity of the UK's apples and conserve them for future generations. The National Fruit Collection based at Brogdale Farm near Faversham in Kent, and maintained by The University of Reading, holds some 2,200 named cultivars in its collection. Apple Day, 21 October, was launched in 1990 by Common Ground – a charity founded to promote local distinctiveness – and Apple Day events now take place across the country throughout the month. Other groups of apple enthusiasts and charities such as The Marcher Apple Network work to revive and protect rare, old varieties.

I hope that the recipes in this book play their part in this important national revival, not only by encouraging you to use this fabulously versatile fruit in different ways but also to seek out and enjoy locally-grown varieties.

1 source: Defra
2 source: National Apple Register of the United Kingdom, 1971.

A Short History of the British Apple

The apple: humble, commonplace and quintessentially British. Or so we like to think. In fact the roots of the edible fruit we know as the apple today are far from British. The apple, it turns out, is something of a globetrotter:

- Almaty, a city in Kazakhstan close to the border with Kyrgyzstan, whose former name, 'Alma-Ata' means 'father of apples' in Kazakh, has long claimed to be the birthplace of the apple. It does so on the basis that the apple's wild ancestor, the *Malus sieversii*, grows in apple forests on the nearby slopes of the Tian Shan mountain range.
- Carl Friedrich von Ledebour, a German-Estonian botanist, first described the *Malus sieversii* in his 1833 work on the flora of the Altay Mountains, *Flora Altaica*. A century later, Nikolai Vavilov, a prominent Russian agronomist known for his work on the origins of cultivated plants, upheld Almaty's claim when he visited the area and was amazed to discover dense forests of wild apple trees.[3]
- Scientists believe Tian Shan apple pips were first transported out of Kazakhstan by Eurasian brown bears long before people began cultivating the fruit. Later, traders travelling to the West along the Silk Road would have eaten the largest, sweetest fruits, starting the process of selection, spreading the pips across Europe and north into the Baltic. From there, new varieties were introduced to Britain by the Romans. Whilst there is evidence to suggest that the European crab apple, the *Malus sylvestris*, grew in Britain during the Neolithic period, the Romans were the first to introduce the larger, sweeter, edible fruits we know today to our shores.
- During the Roman conquest, army veterans were given land on which to grow fruit, as an incentive to settle, and thus the first orchards were established. Subsequent invasions by the Jutes, Saxons and Danes led to many of the orchards being abandoned, but when Christianity was re-introduced in England at the end of the 6th century, monasteries began planting orchards within their grounds. This was followed by the Norman conquest of 1066 which brought varieties such as the Pearmain and Costard from France.

- The Plague, the Wars of the Roses and a series of devastating droughts all led to a downturn in fruit cultivation in the 14th and 15th centuries. This decline was reversed by King Henry VIII when he instructed his fruiterer, Richard Harris (Harrys), to begin an expansion programme, indentifying and introducing new varieties from around the known world. The king was said to have greatly admired apples he had encountered in France so Harris, quite sensibly, chose to import a large number of apple trees from the continent and 'fetched out of France a great store of graftes, especially pippins' along with cherry and pear grafts from the Low Countries. Harris planted Britain's first large-scale orchards in the grounds of his home in Teynham, Kent, and by the end of the 16th century Harris's fruit collection had become 'the chief mother of all other orchards' in England.
- Prior to the British Agricultural Revolution, fruit cultivation was a rather arbitrary process. This changed towards the end of the 18th century when horticulturalist and botanist, Thomas Andrew Knight (later, 2nd President of the Royal Horticultural Society) carried out a series of experiments on pollination. His work influenced many horticulturalists and gardeners of the Victorian era and what followed was an explosion in the development of new apples with head gardeners of country estates, nurserymen and amateur enthusiasts alike competing to produce the finest varieties. Taste was considered to be by far the most important attribute. In a way this proved to be the British apple's undoing as imported fruit – bred for size and yield over taste – began to flood the UK market.

Fortunately, the British apple industry has experienced something of a renaissance in recent years: concerns over the environmental impact of food miles and an increasing dissatisfaction with the bland, homogenised flavour of imported varieties has led to fresh demand for a home-grown produce from both consumers and retailers.

3 Sadly up to 80 per cent of the wild apple trees were cut down for their wood during the Soviet era. The eastern portion of Tian Shan in China was designated as a UNESCO World Heritage Site in 2013 with the western portion in Kazakhstan, Kyrgyzstan and Uzbekistan listed in 2016.

Cooking, Eating, Drinking: Varieties for Different Uses

COOKING

For most culinary uses, it is desirable to use a variety that keeps its shape when cooked. Some examples of this are: Allington Pippin, Annie Elizabeth, Belle de Boskoop, Bountiful, Broadholme Beauty, Calville Blanc d'Hiver, Charles Ross, Galloway Pippin, Howgate Wonder, James Grieve, Lord Hindlip, Mutsu (Crispin), Sanspareil and Scotch Bridget.

PURÉE

For some uses such as ketchups, jams and chutneys, it's desirable for the apple to collapse when cooked. Examples of varieties that cook to a purée are: Alfriston, Arthur Turner, Arthur W. Barnes, Blenheim Orange, Bramley 20, Bramley's Seedling, Catshead, Coeur de Boeuf, Crawley Beauty, Dumelow's Seedling, Edward VII, Emneth Early, Golden Noble, Grenadier, Lane's Prince Albert, Newton Wonder, Peasgood's Nonsuch, Reverend W. Wilks, Scotch Dumpling, Upton Pyne and Yorkshire Greening.

JUICING

Along with orange juice, apple juice is used as the 'base' ingredient for almost all juices and smoothies. Some of the best varieties for juicing are: Ashmead's Kernel, Bramley 20, Bramley's Seedling, Cox's Orange Pippin, Cripps Pink (Pink Lady®), D'Arcy Spice, Discovery, Egremont Russet, Greensleeves, Grenadier, Howgate Wonder, James Grieve, Lane's Prince Albert, Lord Lambourne, Mutsu (Crispin), Spartan, Tydeman's Late Orange and Worcester Pearmain.

SALADS

Sweet/sharp varieties work particularly well in salads. Try Ashmead's Kernel, Brownlees' Russet, Chivers Delight, Christmas Pippin®, Cox's Orange Pippin, Cripps Pink (Pink Lady®), Discovery, Egremont

Russet, Fearn's Pippin, Gladstone, Golden Harvey, Greensleeves, Kidd's Orange Red, Maclean's Favourite, Miller's Seedling, Norfolk Royal, Opal (Seabrook), Rubinette, Sanspareil, Sturmer Pippin or Tydeman's Early Worcester.

STORING APPLES

Early-season apples generally do not keep well and ideally should be eaten within 1–2 days of being picked.

Mid-season apples will usually keep for 2–3 weeks, if stored in the refrigerator.

Late-season apples generally keep the longest. Most can be stored in a cellar, frost-proof garden shed or another cool, dark place with good ventilation for 6–8 weeks. A good keeping variety will keep well into the new year and beyond if stored in the right conditions.

The flavour of fruits will continue to develop in storage. Acidity will drop and sugar levels will increase, meaning that fruits will taste sweeter and cook more firmly after being stored for a time.

Key points for storing apples:

- If you are picking apples with the intention of storing them, it's best to pick them slightly under-ripe as fruits will continue to mature in storage.
- Before storing, check that the fruits are dry and completely blemish-free. Bruised fruit will go off especially quickly.
- Apples are best stored on wooden or chicken-wire shelves. This allows air to circulate around the fruit. Some experts further recommend using shredded newspaper, straw or cardboard liners to separate the fruit and keep any moisture in check.
- Do not allow fruits to touch, or rot, when it sets in, will spread like wildfire to neighbouring fruit.
- Check the fruit regularly and remove any that are starting to go off.

Flavour Combinations

Apples pair well with so many different ingredients. This list, although by no means exhaustive, shows some of the winning ways with this wonderfully versatile fruit:

FRUITS
Blackberry
Blackcurrant
Chilli pepper
Cranberry
Date
Kiwi fruit
Lemon
Lime
Mango
Nectarine
Orange
Passion fruit
Peach
Pear
Pineapple
Plum
Pomegranate
Quince
Raspberry
Redcurrant
Rhubarb
Strawberry
Tomato

DRIED FRUITS
Prune
Raisin
Sultana

VEGETABLES
Beetroot
Brussels sprouts
Cabbage
Cauliflower
Carrot
Celeriac
Celery
Chicory
Leek
Onion
Parsnip
Pea
Pumpkin
Shallot
Spinach
Spring onion
Squash
Swede
Sweet potato

HERBS
Coriander
Fennel
Mint
Rosemary
Sage
Thyme

SPICES
Allspice
Anise
Black pepper
Cardamom
Cinnamon
Clove
Cumin
Ginger
Juniper
Lavender
Mace
Nutmeg
Saffron
Vanilla

NUTS
Almond
Chestnut
Hazelnut
Peanut
Pecan
Pistachio
Walnut

GRAINS & PULSES
Oats
Puy lentils

CHEESES	MEATS	FISH & SEAFOOD	SUGARS
Blue cheese	Beef	Cod	Brown Sugar
Brie	Chicken	Crab	Caramel
Cheddar	Duck	Herring	Honey
Cream cheese	Pork	Mackerel	Marzipan
Edam	Turkey	Trout	
Goat's cheese		Tuna	**ALCOHOL**
Gruyère			Amaretto
Mascarpone			Brandy
			Calvados
			Cider
			Rum

CHEESE & APPLE PAIRING

Cheese and apple are a match made in heaven. There aren't any set rules but as a general principle: the stronger the cheese, the sharper the apple.

Mild-flavoured, sweet varieties go well with soft, cream cheeses; well-flavoured sweet-sharp varieties pair with medium strength cheeses; and tart varieties hold up best against blue cheeses.

Blue cheese: Granny Smith, Howgate Wonder, Lady Hollendale
Brie, Camembert, Gruyère: Ambrosia, Captain Kidd, Kidd's Orange Red, Laxton's Superb, Sanspareil
Cheddar: Ashmead's Kernel, Cox's Orange Pippin, Epicure, Gala, George Cave, Maclean's Favourite, Sturmer Pippin, Zari®
Cream cheese: Ben's Red, Greensleeves, Laxton's Fortune
Emmental: Charles Ross, Pink Lady® (Cripps Pink), Sundowner®
Goat's cheese: Gala, Kanzi®, Rubens®
Gouda: Braeburn, Egremont Russet, Ribston Pippin
Mascarpone: Broadholme Beauty, Devonshire Quarrenden, Discovery, Jonagold, Tydeman's Early Worcester, Worcester Pearmain
Mozzarella: Admiral, Ball's Pippin, Sunrise, Cox's Orange Pippin

BASIC RECIPES

Basic Vegetable Stock

MAKES: ABOUT I LITRE • PREP TIME: 15 MINUTES • COOK TIME: 15–20 MINUTES

A simple vegetable stock acts as a savoury base for a range of soups, stews and other recipes. Shop-bought stock cubes tend to be very salty and lack flavour. With this recipe you can vary the ingredients according to taste – the objective is to create a light broth to complement and add depth of flavour to a dish but not overpower it.

I tbsp olive oil
I onion, diced
I leek, washed, trimmed
   and thinly sliced
I carrot, diced
3 garlic cloves, unpeeled,
   bashed

2 celery sticks, washed and
   thinly sliced
10 button mushrooms (optional)
2–3 tomatoes, diced (optional)
2 tsp whole black peppercorns
2–3 bay leaves
2–3 sprigs of thyme or parsley

1 Add the olive oil to a large heavy-based saucepan and set over a medium heat.
2 Add the onion, leek and carrot and sweat for 2–3 minutes.
3 Add enough cold water to generously cover the vegetables and increase the heat.
4 Stir in the rest of the ingredients. Bring to the boil, cover, and boil gently for 15 minutes.
5 Remove from the heat and pour the stock through a sieve. Discard the vegetables or save for another use. The liquid stock is now ready to be used. *Store, covered, in the fridge for up to 4 days or freeze in batches and use within 4 months.*

Basic Shortcrust Pastry

SERVES: 4 • PREP TIME: 10 MINUTES • COOK TIME: 20–25 MINUTES

This is the basic savoury pastry, but if you want to make a sweet shortcrust pastry for a dessert, just add 2–3 tablespoons of caster sugar. To give your pastry an extra lift, you can add ground spices, fruit peel, chopped nuts, freshly chopped herbs or finely grated cheese to the basic recipe.

MAKES 300G PASTRY OR ENOUGH FOR A 23CM (9 INCH) SINGLE-CRUST PIE	MAKES 450G PASTRY OR ENOUGH FOR A 23CM (9 INCH) DOUBLE-CRUST PIE
200g plain flour, plus extra for dusting	300g plain flour, plus extra for dusting
Pinch of salt	Pinch of salt
50g butter, cubed, plus extra for greasing	75g butter, cubed, plus extra for greasing
50g vegetable fat (such as Trex or Cookeen), cubed	75g vegetable fat (such as Trex or Cookeen), cubed
2–3 tbsp cold water, more if needed	4–5 tbsp cold water, more if needed

1 Sift the flour into a large bowl and add a pinch of salt. Use your fingertips to rub in the butter and vegetable shortening until the mixture resembles fine breadcrumbs.
2 Add the water, 1 tablespoon at a time, stirring it in with a knife. When the dough is just moist enough to hold together, knead it lightly to form a ball – a few presses to bring it together is all you need, don't be tempted to overwork the dough.
3 Wrap the dough tightly in cling film (this prevents it drying out) and put it in the fridge for at least 30 minutes before use. Chilling the dough helps to stabilise it and minimise shrinkage in the oven. *The dough can be left in the fridge for up to 2 days or in the freezer sealed in a large plastic bag for up to 3 months. Before using frozen dough, thaw overnight in the fridge and remove about 30 minutes before rolling. The pastry will crack if it is too cold.*

TIPS

The key to perfect, crumbly shortcrust pastry is to keep handling to a minimum. The more the dough is manipulated, the more stringy gluten protein forms and the tougher and chewier the pastry will be. Although some gluten formation is unavoidable (without it the pastry would be too 'short' to hold together), over-working it will strengthen the strands of gluten. So, as soon as the dough forms a ball, stop kneading. Don't be tempted to keep going. Crumbly, buttery goodness is where it's at.

Vegetable shortening and lard contain less water than butter, so by using half vegetable shortening, half butter you will get a crumblier, flakier pastry.

ℬREADCRUMBS

PREP TIME: 5 MINUTES ● COOK TIME: 15–20 MINUTES

Breadcrumbs are a great way to use up bread that is past its prime. Add herbs or spices to create your own seasoned crumbs.

2–3 slices of day-old bread

1 Preheat the oven to 140°C/120°C fan/gas mark 1.
2 Cut the crusts off the bread and tear it into 2.5cm (1-inch) pieces.
3 Spread the pieces out in a single layer on a baking sheet.
4 Bake until the bread is dry and just beginning to turn golden brown, about 20 minutes – less if the bread is a couple of days old.
5 Remove from the oven and allow the toasted bread to cool.
6 Tip into a sealable plastic bag and use a rolling pin to slowly crush the bread into crumbs. Alternatively, transfer the baked bread to a food processor and blitz until the pieces have reduced to crumbs.

SPRING

Apple, Pea & Ham Soup

SERVES: 4 • PREP TIME: 10 MINUTES • COOK TIME: 20–25 MINUTES

Vibrant apple, pea and ham soup is a great way to start a spring meal.

2 tbsp butter
I medium floury potato, such as
    Desiree or Maris Piper, peeled
    and diced
Small bunch of spring onions,
    coarsely chopped
2 garlic cloves, minced
I litre vegetable stock (see page 15)
3 medium well-flavoured dessert
    apples (try Ashmead's Kernel,
    Court Pendu Plat, Cox's Orange
    Pippin or Lord Hindlip)

300g petit pois
Good pinch of caster sugar
I tbsp fresh lemon juice
120g cooked bacon lardons
150ml soured cream
Sea salt and freshly ground
    black pepper, to taste

EQUIPMENT
Hand blender or blender

1 Melt the butter in a large, heavy-based saucepan over a medium heat.
   Add the potato, spring onions, garlic and stock. Bring to the boil, then
   reduce to a medium heat and simmer for 15 minutes, until the potato
   is very tender.
2 Peel, core and coarsely chop the apples and add to the pan. Add the
   peas and simmer for 4–5 minutes.
3 Remove from the heat and stir in the sugar and lemon juice. Transfer
   to a blender or whizz with a hand blender until smooth.
4 Return the soup to the saucepan, add the lardons, then stir in half of
   the soured cream. Season with salt and black pepper, to taste.
5 Return the pan to the hob and gently warm the soup through, taking
   care not to let it boil (as this may cause the soured cream to curdle).
6 Serve immediately swirled with the remaining soured cream.

APPLE-LARDON TOASTS WITH FENNEL

SERVES: 4 • PREP TIME: 10 MINUTES • COOK TIME: 2–4 MINUTES

This sweet and savoury snack is so simple but oh-so tasty.

1 loaf crusty bread, preferably
  ciabatta or baguette
2 tbsp extra-virgin olive oil,
  to brush
2 garlic cloves, sliced in half
  on the diagonal

2 medium dessert apples
  (try Cameo®, Cox's Orange
  Pippin or Gala)
240g cooked bacon lardons
1 tsp fennel seeds, lightly crushed
Salt and freshly ground black pepper

1 Preheat the grill to medium and line the grill pan with foil. Position
  the grill rack 7.5–10cm (3–4 inches) from the heat source.
2 Slice the bread diagonally into 12 thick slices. Toast until light brown
  on both sides.
3 Remove from the grill and brush with olive oil. Gently rub the cut side
  of a garlic clove over the toasts.
4 Peel, core and very finely chop the apples. Add to a small bowl and
  combine with the lardons.
5 Spoon the bacon and apple mixture onto the toasts and sprinkle
  with fennel seeds. Season with freshly ground black pepper, to taste.
  Serve immediately.

Asian Fish with Cider Sabayon

SERVES: 4 • PREP TIME: 20 MINUTES • COOK TIME: 20 MINUTES

Steamed fish makes a fantastic low-fat meal.

1 medium dessert apple
(try Braeburn, Fuji or Gala)
100g pak choi, sliced
1 red pepper, deseeded and
finely sliced
4 × 150g fillets firm white fish
2 garlic cloves, minced
5cm (2-inch) piece fresh root
ginger, peeled and finely grated
2 tsp rice vinegar
Salt and freshly ground black
pepper, to taste

Small bunch of spring onions,
finely chopped
Handful of coriander, chopped

CIDER SABAYON

3 egg yolks
150ml dry English cider
Salt and freshly ground black
pepper, to taste
Tabasco® sauce, to taste (optional)

Noodles, to serve

1 Heat the oven to 200°C/180°C fan/gas mark 6. Lay a large rectangle of foil on a baking sheet.
2 Wash, core and thinly slice the apple and arrange the slices down the centre of the foil. Add the pak choi and red pepper.
3 Place the fish on top and sprinkle over the garlic and ginger. Drizzle with rice vinegar and season to taste.
4 Fold the foil over and seal the edges to make a parcel. Bake for 20 minutes.
5 Meanwhile, make the cider sabayon. Heat a saucepan of water until lightly simmering.
6 Add the egg yolks and cider to a medium bowl and whisk for 1 minute. Place the bowl over the pan and whisk constantly for 7–8 minutes, until light and fluffy. The sabayon is ready when it is thick enough to coat the back of a spoon. Season to taste and add a splash of Tabasco®, if you like.
7 Transfer the cooked fish fillets to four plates, resting them on a bed of noodles, then spoon over the cider sabayon and sprinkle with the spring onions and coriander.

Potato & Apple Rösti Cake

SERVES: 6–8 • PREP TIME: 20–30 MINUTES •
COOK TIME: 1 HOUR 25 MINUTES

This potato and apple hash brown-style cake is soft and creamy on the inside and crisp on the outside. All that grating may seem like a bit of a faff but it's worth the effort.

1 tbsp butter, plus extra for greasing
6 rashers back bacon
1.25kg floury potatoes (such as Desiree, King Edward or Maris Piper), peeled, left whole
4 tbsp olive oil
2 medium dessert apples (try Cameo®, Cox's Orange Pippin or Gala)
1 small onion, finely chopped

1 Heat the oven to 190°C/170°C fan/gas mark 5. Place a baking sheet in the oven to warm through. Generously grease a 20cm (8 inch) loose-bottomed cake tin with butter.

2 Add the bacon to a dry frying pan and cook for 5 minutes, until crisp, then remove and cut into small pieces.

3 Add the potatoes to a saucepan of cold water. Bring to the boil, then reduce the heat and simmer for 10 minutes, until parboiled yet still firm. Drain, then, place in a bowl of chilled water.

4 When cool enough to handle, pat the potatoes dry with kitchen paper and coarsely grate into a large bowl. Add the olive oil and toss well to prevent the potatoes sticking.

5 Peel, core and roughly grate the apples. Squeeze out any excess juice from the grated apples and chopped onion and add to the potato. Scatter over the bacon and stir well to combine.

6 Add the potato mixture to the prepared baking tin, taking care not to pack it too densely, and dot with small pieces of the butter.

7 Place on the hot baking sheet and cook for 1 hour 10 minutes, until cooked through and crispy and brown on top. Allow the rösti to cool in the tin before transferring to a serving plate. Serve on its own as a tasty snack, or with a side salad as a light meal.

₭orean ₵itrus ₱ork ₴kewers with ₨oasted ₳pple

MAKES: 4 LARGE SKEWERS • PREP TIME: 20 MINUTES,
PLUS MARINATING • COOK TIME: 30–35 MINUTES

The sweetness of roasted apples combines wonderfully well with pork and here the subtle heat of the chilli in the citrus marinade adds a little kick and a depth of flavour.

For a main course, serve with some crisp lettuce leaves, finely chopped spring onion and rice.

225g lean pork loin, cut into
    20 2.5cm (1-inch) cubes
3 medium sweet dessert apples (try
    Pink Lady®/Cripps Pink or Fuji)
Butter, for greasing
1 tsp granulated sugar
½ tsp ground cinnamon
Salt and white pepper, to taste

CITRUS MARINADE
4 tbsp kimchi (available in larger
    supermarkets)

2 tbsp rice vinegar
3 tbsp soy sauce
Juice of ½ orange
2 tbsp extra-virgin olive oil
Salt and white pepper,
    to taste

EQUIPMENT
4 skewers – if using bamboo,
    soak in cold water for
    30 minutes before use to
    prevent them burning

1 First make the marinade. Add the kimchi, rice vinegar, soy sauce and orange juice to the bowl of a food processor and blend until smooth. Whisk in the oil and season well with salt and white pepper.
2 Add the pork to a bowl and pour over the marinade. Stir to coat. Cover with cling film and place in the fridge for at least 30 minutes, preferably 5–6 hours, to marinate.
3 Heat the oven to 170°C/150°C fan/gas mark 3. Peel, core and slice the apples in half. Grease a baking sheet with butter. Arrange the apples in a single layer and sprinkle with the sugar and cinnamon.

4 Bake for 15 minutes, until the apples are just tender. Remove from
   the oven and set aside to cool.
5 To assemble the skewers, slice the roasted apple halves into 4 so that
   you have 24 pieces in total. On each skewer, thread the roasted apple
   and marinated pork, alternating between the two.
6 Set a griddle pan over a medium-high heat. Cook the skewers for
   3–4 minutes on each side, or until the pork is brown. Season to taste
   with salt and white pepper and serve immediately.

NOTE

Kimchi is a traditional Korean side dish made from salted fermented
vegetables, most commonly Napa cabbage and daikon radish, seasoned
with chilli, garlic and ginger. Fermented cabbage may not sound that
appetising – and it doesn't smell too promising when you open the jar
either(!) – but it tastes great.

THAI CHICKEN & APPLE SALAD WITH PEANUT DRESSING

SERVES: 4 AS A LIGHT MEAL, 6 AS A SIDE •
PREP TIME: 20 MINUTES • COOK TIME: 2 MINUTES

This simple Asian-inspired salad is packed with flavour and couldn't be easier to make.

DRESSING
3 tbsp extra-virgin olive oil
2 tbsp rice vinegar
2 tbsp soy sauce
2 tbsp crunchy peanut butter
2 tbsp Thai sweet chilli sauce
1 garlic clove, minced
Juice of ½ lime

SALAD
150g beansprouts
1 well-flavoured dessert apple
    (try Braeburn, Cox or Gala)

120g salad leaves (a combination
    of rocket, mizuna and spinach
    works well)
½ cucumber, deseeded and cut
    into thin strips
Small bunch of spring onions,
    finely chopped
½ red pepper, deseeded and cut
    into thin strips
200g cooked skinless chicken
    breast mini fillets
1 tbsp toasted sesame seeds,
    to garnish

1 Add the beansprouts to a saucepan of boiling water and cook for a minute or so. Drain then set aside to cool.
2 To make the dressing, pour all the ingredients into a screwtop jar. Shake vigorously until the peanut butter is well blended, then set aside.
3 Wash, quarter, core and thinly slice the apple, peel on, and add to a large bowl along with the beansprouts, salad leaves, cucumber, spring onion and red pepper. Toss well to combine.
4 Slice the cooked chicken into small chunks and scatter over the top.
5 Shake the dressing again. Drizzle a little dressing over the salad and lightly toss. Serve sprinkled with toasted sesame seeds and the remainder of the dressing in a jug alongside.

ASIAN APPLE SALAD WITH YUZU-STYLE CITRUS DRESSING

SERVES: 4 • PREP TIME: 10–15 MINUTES

This Japanese-inspired apple salad couldn't be simpler and the Yuzu dressing adds a lovely light, citrusy zing. Yuzu Citrus Sauce is now available in bottles in larger supermarkets but homemade always tastes better.

For a more substantial salad try adding some flaked tuna or salmon and soba noodles. (See the photo for this recipe on page 18.)

YUZU-STYLE CITRUS DRESSING

Makes about 150ml

Juice of I clementine
Juice of I lime
2 tbsp extra-virgin olive oil
I tbsp rice vinegar
I tbsp soy sauce
I garlic clove, minced
½ tsp finely grated fresh ginger
2 tsp dark brown soft sugar

SALAD

2 crisp, sweet dessert apples (try Pink Lady®/Cripps Pink or Fuji)

4 medium carrots, peeled and sliced into matchsticks (I find it easiest to use a mandolin but if you haven't got one, just coarsely grate them)
I red pepper, deseeded and thinly sliced
I small red onion, finely chopped
100g beansprouts, washed
60g sultanas
I small red chilli, deseeded and very finely chopped
Small handful of coriander, roughly chopped

1 To make the dressing, pour all the ingredients into a small, screwtop jar. Shake to combine, then set aside.
2 Wash and slice the apples into thin matchsticks (again, coarsely grated is fine, too) and add to a large bowl along with the carrots, pepper, onion, beansprouts, sultanas and chilli.
3 Shake the dressing again and drizzle 3 tablespoonfuls over the salad. Stir the coriander through just before serving. *Store the leftover Yuzu-style Citrus Dressing in a sealed jar in the fridge and use within 2 weeks.*

BRAMLEY APPLE KETCHUP

MAKES: 1 JAR (ABOUT 500ML) • PREP TIME: 10 MINUTES •
COOK TIME: 2 HOURS 10 MINUTES

2 tbsp vegetable or olive oil
2 large onions, finely chopped
1.5kg Bramley apples
175g caster sugar
200ml malt vinegar
Pinch of ground cayenne
    pepper
Pinch of ground allspice

Salt and freshly ground
    black pepper, to season
6 whole cloves
1 cinnamon stick

EQUIPMENT
Small square of muslin
Hand blender or blender

1 Heat the oil in a large heavy-based saucepan over a low heat. Add
   the onions and sweat until soft and translucent, about 10 minutes.
   Meanwhile, wash, core and finely chop the apples, peel on.
2 Add the apple and stir in the sugar, vinegar, cayenne pepper and
   allspice. Season with salt and black pepper and stir well.
3 Add the cloves and cinnamon to a small square of muslin and tie the
   top before adding to the pan.
4 Simmer, uncovered, over a low heat for 1½–2 hours, stirring occasionally,
   until the mixture has reduced to a glossy pulp. Remove from the heat
   and discard the spice bag. Whizz with a hand blender until smooth,
   then pass through a sieve into a bowl. (The ketchup will thicken slightly
   as it cools). Spoon into a hot, sterilised jar (see below) and seal. *Store in
   a cool, dry place for up to 6 months. Once opened, store in the fridge.*

HOW TO STERILISE GLASS JARS

1 First, wash the jars and lids thoroughly in hot, soapy water. Rinse
   and place upside down on a baking tray. Dry in an oven heated to
   150°C/130°C fan/gas mark 2 for 10 minutes.
2 Fill while the mixture and jars are still hot. Be careful not to touch or
   get any of the mixture on the rim as this could introduce bacteria.

Mini Apple Doughnuts with Fresh Lime Curd

MAKES: 12 BITE-SIZED DOUGHNUTS • PREP TIME: 20 MINUTES,
PLUS 2 HOURS 30 MINUTES PROVING • COOK TIME: 35 MINUTES

Fresh lime curd adds a delicious zing to these bite-sized delights.

DOUGHNUTS
90ml milk
2 tbsp butter, plus extra for
   greasing
100g tart apples (try Annie Elizabeth
   or Cottenham Seedling)
240g plain flour, plus extra for
   dusting
1 scant tsp fast-action dried yeast
¼ tsp salt
2 tbsp golden caster sugar, plus
   1 tbsp for dusting
¼ tsp ground cinnamon, plus extra
   for dusting
¼ tsp grated nutmeg, plus extra
   for dusting
1 egg, beaten

2 × 250g blocks vegetable fat
   (such as Trex or Cookeen) or
   enough vegetable oil to fill a
   large saucepan to a depth of
   at least 5cm (2 inches) with
   10cm (4 inches) space above

FRESH LIME CURD
Finely grated zest and juice of
   1 unwaxed lime
55g golden caster sugar
1 tbsp cold unsalted butter
1 large egg, lightly beaten

EQUIPMENT
Sugar thermometer, optional
Piping bag fitted with a small nozzle

1 To make the doughnuts: warm the milk in a small saucepan over a
   medium-low heat. Add the butter and set aside until the milk has
   cooled to hand temperature and the butter has melted.
2 Peel, core and coarsely grate the apples.
3 Sift the flour into a large bowl and stir in the yeast, salt, sugar,
   cinnamon and nutmeg. Make a well in the centre and pour in the
   warm milk mixture, egg and grated apple. Stir with a wooden spoon
   and then turn out onto a floured surface. Knead for a couple of minutes
   to combine. Add the dough to a lightly oiled bowl, cover with oiled

cling film and place it in a warm, draught-free area until the dough has doubled in size, about 2 hours.

4 Meanwhile, make the curd. Add the lime juice, sugar, butter and egg to a small saucepan. Cook over a medium-low heat. Whisk frequently and vigorously, until the mixture has thickened like custard and holds the marks of a whisk drawn across the surface, about 15 minutes.

5 Place a fine mesh sieve over a bowl and press the curd through using the back of a spoon. Stir in the lime zest and set aside to cool.

6 Lightly grease 2 large baking sheets. Uncover the dough and punch down to knock out all the air. Take a lump of dough, roughly the size of a walnut, and roll it into a ball. (The dough will be very sticky so it helps to flour your hands.) Place the dough ball on a baking sheet and gently flatten using the palm of your hand. Repeat with the remaining dough – spacing the balls at least 5cm (2 inches) apart on the baking sheets. Cover the baking sheets with oiled cling film and set aside to prove until doubled in size again, about 30 minutes.

7 Place a couple of sheets of kitchen paper on a large plate. On another plate, mix together the tablespoon of caster sugar and a pinch of cinnamon and nutmeg and set both plates aside.

8 Melt the vegetable fat in a large heavy-based saucepan over a high heat. If you have a sugar thermometer, the temperature should reach 180°C. If you don't, drop in a small piece of bread – the oil is ready when it browns in about 30 seconds. Drop 3 or 4 doughnuts in at a time and cook for 5–6 minutes until each one is puffed and a deep, golden brown. Remove from the pan using a slotted spoon. Drain on the kitchen paper then toss in the sugar, cinnamon and nutmeg.

9 To fill the doughnuts, use a skewer to make a hole in the side of each one. Jiggle it around to create a cavity in the middle. Fill a piping bag fitted with a small nozzle with the curd, then insert into the doughnut and squeeze in the filling. Repeat with the remaining doughnuts. Then enjoy!

TIP
Fresh lime curd can be made up to a week in advance. Cover the surface of the curd with cling film, seal the jar and store in the fridge.

Green Apple & Lemon Sherbet with Mint

SERVES: 4 • PREP TIME: 40–45 MINUTES, INCLUDING
30 MINUTES INFUSING • CHILLING TIME: 20–25 MINUTES

This bright, iced dessert is a refreshing, light way to end a meal.

240ml cold water
200g caster sugar
Small bunch of mint
800g tart green apples (Granny
    Smith work well)

Zest and juice of 1 unwaxed lemon
120ml milk

EQUIPMENT
Ice cream maker

1 Add the water and sugar to a small saucepan and cook over a
   medium-low heat, stirring constantly, until the sugar has fully
   dissolved. Remove from the heat then add the whole mint sprigs,
   reserving a few leaves for garnish. Set aside for at least 30 minutes
   to allow the flavour of the mint to infuse.
2 Wash, core and chop the apples into small pieces, peel on, and
   immediately toss in the lemon juice to prevent browning. Transfer
   the chopped apple and lemon juice to the bowl of a food processor
   and blend until smooth.
3 Place a fine-mesh sieve over a large bowl and press the fruit purée
   through using the back of a spoon. Discard any pulp left behind and
   rinse out the sieve.
4 Strain the mint syrup into the bowl, pressing lightly on the mint with
   the back of a spoon. Discard the mint.
5 Add the milk and lemon zest and whisk to fully combine.
6 Transfer to the bowl of an ice cream maker and freeze according to
   the manufacturer's instructions. If you don't have an ice cream maker
   see *No ice cream maker? No worries* overleaf.

continued

7 Best served immediately after churning for a meltingly soft texture (after that, ice crystals begin to form and the sorbet becomes slightly grainy).

8 Serve garnished with the reserved mint leaves.

VARIATION

For a more sophisticated flavour, try orange, apple and basil or apple with a hint of fresh rosemary or thyme and a splash of vodka. Don't go overboard with the booze, though – a tablespoonful will suffice. Too much alcohol will prevent the sorbet freezing.

No Ice Cream Maker? No Worries

If you don't have the space, or budget, for an ice cream maker, fear not, with a little extra effort and some elbow grease you can still make delicious homemade iced treats. Here's how:

1 Prepare the fruit and yoghurt or ice cream base following the recipe steps. Pour the fruit purée into the base in a freezerproof container with a lid and whisk together until fully combined.

2 Next prepare an ice bath by filling a large bowl (or sink) with ice and cold tap water – just enough to allow the ice to float around freely without sticking together – and a couple of tablespoonfuls of salt (the salt helps to speed up the chilling process). Lower the tub of yoghurt/ice cream mixture into the ice bath and leave to chill for 10–15 minutes before popping the lid on and transferring it to the freezer.

3 Check the mixture after 30 minutes. Once ice crystals start to form around the edges, remove the tub from the freezer and beat firmly with a whisk to break them up as much as possible.

4 Return it to the freezer and repeat the process every 30 minutes or so until the frozen yoghurt or ice cream has reached the desired consistency (usually after 2–2½ hours).

Apple & Spinach Smoothie

SERVES: 2 • PREP TIME: 5 MINUTES

This healthy green smoothie is packed with nutrients and tastes pretty good too. See page 10 for a note on the best varieties to use for juicing.

5cm (2 inch) piece cucumber, diced
1 celery stick, washed, trimmed and
    chopped
Good handful of baby spinach

100ml apple juice, chilled
1 small ripe banana, peeled
    and sliced
Juice of 1 lime

1 Add all the ingredients to the bowl of a food processor and blend until smooth. Dilute with a little cold water, if desired, then pour into glasses and serve.

NOTE
Adding banana thickens and adds creaminess to the smoothie but if, like me, you're not nuts about 'nana you can substitute it with half an avocado, 2 tbsp ground oatmeal, chia seeds or milled flaxseeds.

FRESH APPLETINI

SERVES: 2 • PREP TIME: 5 MINUTES •
COOK TIME: 3 MINUTES, PLUS COOLING

2 medium-to-large apples (a juicy, sweet-tart, late-keeping variety such as Ashmead's Kernel, Howgate Wonder, Lane's Prince Albert, or Newton Wonder would be ideal)

65ml Homemade Simple Syrup (see below)
Juice of ½ lemon
80ml vodka
Ice

1 First make the simple syrup following the instructions below. Place 2 martini glasses in the freezer to chill while you make the drinks.
2 Peel, quarter, core and finely chop the apples. Add to the bowl of a food processor along with the simple syrup and lemon juice and blend until smooth.
3 Pour the apple purée and vodka into a cocktail shaker filled with a little ice and shake vigorously until the exterior is frosty.
4 Strain into 2 chilled martini glasses and garnish with a few apple slices secured with a clove, if desired. Get busy.

HOMEMADE SIMPLE SYRUP

MAKES: 200ML • COOK TIME: 10 MINUTES

100ml water
100g granulated sugar

1 Heat 100ml water in a medium saucepan over a medium-low heat until the water is hot, but not boiling. Add the sugar and stir until it has fully dissolved.
2 Remove from the heat and allow the syrup to cool to room temperature before use. *Store in a sealed jar in the fridge for up to 3 weeks.*

SUMMER

CHILLED CURRIED APPLE SOUP

SERVES: 4 • PREP TIME: 10 MINUTES •
COOK TIME: 30–35 MINUTES, PLUS CHILLING

This refreshing soup has a hint of spice and citrus – perfect for summer. I like to use Fuji apples for this; they're naturally very sweet and juicy and their flavour holds up well against the curry powder. (See the photo for this recipe on page 14.)

3–4 sweet dessert apples, about 600g (try Fuji, Gladstone or Laxton's Early Crimson)
Juice of 1 small lemon
2 tbsp butter
1 medium onion, coarsely chopped
Sea salt and freshly ground black pepper, to taste
2 tsp mild curry powder
½ tsp ground cumin, plus extra to serve

1 tsp finely grated fresh root ginger
1 litre vegetable (see page 15) or chicken stock
125ml single cream
4–6 sprigs of watercress, to garnish (optional)
Wedges of toasted pitta bread brushed with olive oil, to serve

EQUIPMENT
Hand blender or blender

1 Peel, core and coarsely chop the apples and immediately toss into a bowl with the lemon juice to prevent browning.
2 Melt the butter in a large heavy-based saucepan over a medium heat. Add the onion and cook gently for 5–6 minutes, stirring occasionally, until soft and translucent. Reduce the heat if the onion starts to brown. Season lightly with salt and black pepper.
3 Add the curry powder, cumin and ginger to the pan and cook for another 2 minutes, stirring occasionally.
4 Add the stock, chopped apple – along with the lemon juice – to the pan. Cover and bring to the boil, then reduce the heat and simmer for 25 minutes, until the apple is very tender.

5 Remove from the heat and set aside to cool for a few minutes. Transfer to a blender or whizz with a hand blender until smooth then pass through a sieve into a large bowl. Cover with cling film and chill in the fridge for at least 3 hours.

6 Stir in most of the cream and check for seasoning. Serve with a swirl of cream and garnish with a sprig of watercress, if you like.

7 Delicious served with toasted pitta bread wedges, brushed with olive oil and lightly sprinkled with ground cumin and a pinch of sea salt.

TIP

This soup is just as tasty served hot. After blending, pass through a sieve into the rinsed-out pan and reheat over a medium-low heat, stirring occasionally. Remove from the heat and serve immediately.

APPLE COLESLAW

SERVES: 6–8 • PREP TIME: 20 MINUTES, PLUS 10–15 MINUTES RESTING

This fresh and flavoursome homemade coleslaw beats shop-bought versions hands down.

1 medium sweet dessert apple
  (try Discovery or Laxton's
  Early Crimson)
1 medium tart dessert apple
  (try Epicure, Feltham Beauty
  or Lady Hollendale)
1 tbsp lemon juice
225g white cabbage, finely
  shredded

1 large carrot, peeled and
  coarsely grated
1 celery stick, finely chopped
2 spring onions, finely chopped
6 tbsp mayonnaise
2 tbsp white wine vinegar
6 tbsp dark brown soft sugar
Salt and freshly ground
  black pepper, to taste

1 Wash, quarter, core and finely chop the apples and add to a large bowl. Immediately toss in the lemon juice to prevent browning. Add the cabbage, carrot, celery and spring onions.
2 Combine the mayonnaise, vinegar and sugar in a small bowl and then pour over the chopped salad. Toss to coat, then season to taste.
3 Set aside for 10–15 minutes to allow the flavours to meld before serving.

TIP

For a lighter dressing, replace the mayonnaise with natural yoghurt and add a little extra lemon juice to boost the flavour.

$\mathcal{A}$PPLE $\mathcal{S}$ALSA

SERVES: 4–6 • PREP TIME: 10 MINUTES

A fresh and zingy alternative to traditional tomato salsa. Great served as a dip with tortillas or toasted pitta bread strips, or as an accompaniment to chicken, pork or beef Tex-Mex.

2 medium well-flavoured dessert
    apples (try Beauty of Bath,
    Epicure or Gladstone)
Juice of ½ lime
½ small red onion, very finely
    chopped
½ green pepper, deseeded and
    very finely chopped

½ tsp cayenne pepper
Small splash of white
    wine vinegar
½ bunch of coriander,
    roughly chopped
Salt and freshly ground
    black pepper, to taste

1 Wash, quarter, core and very finely chop the apples, with the peel on, and add to a bowl. Immediately toss in the lime juice to prevent browning. Then add the onion, green pepper, cayenne pepper, vinegar and coriander. Season, then toss to combine.
2 Refrigerate until needed.

Apple & Red Pepper Stuffing

SERVES: 4 (2 STUFFING BALLS PER PERSON) •
PREP TIME: 15 MINUTES • COOK TIME: 40–45 MINUTES

These moreish little stuffing balls are a welcome addition to chicken or turkey dishes.

2 tbsp olive oil, plus extra for greasing

1 medium dessert apple (a sweet-sharp variety such as Beauty of Bath, George Cave or Gladstone would work well)

1 red pepper, deseeded and finely chopped

1 small red onion, finely chopped

1 garlic clove, minced

3 slices wholemeal bread, made into breadcrumbs (see page 17)

3 tbsp apple juice

½ tsp dried thyme

Salt and freshly ground pepper, to taste

1 egg, beaten

1 Preheat the oven to 180°C/160°C fan/gas mark 4. Grease a baking sheet with a little oil.

2 Peel, quarter, core and finely chop the apple.

3 Heat the oil in a frying pan and add the apple, pepper, onion and garlic. Cook over a medium heat for 10 minutes. Remove from the heat and set aside to cool for a few minutes.

4 Add the apple mixture to a large bowl along with the breadcrumbs, apple juice and thyme and season to taste.

5 Add the egg and stir to thoroughly combine.

6 Scoop out walnut-sized chunks of stuffing, roll into 8 small balls and place on the prepared baking sheet.

7 Bake for 30–35 minutes, until golden and crispy.

VARIATION

If serving alongside roast lamb or beef, try substituting the red pepper with 50g dried apricots.

Sun-dried Tomato, Cheddar & Apple Muffins

MAKES: 8 LARGE OR 12 CUPCAKE-SIZED MUFFINS •
PREP TIME: 15 MINUTES • COOK TIME: 20–25 MINUTES

Savoury muffins are perfect for picnics or lunchboxes. The apple in this recipe adds moisture as well as flavour.

2 eggs
225g self-raising flour
50g plain flour
1 tsp baking powder
¼ tsp salt
½ level tsp bicarbonate of soda
100ml milk
125ml Greek yoghurt

1 medium well-flavoured dessert apple (try Epicure, Feltham Beauty or George Cave)
100g mature Cheddar cheese, coarsely grated
50g sun-dried tomatoes, chopped
2 tsp dried oregano
100g butter, melted

1 Preheat the oven to 200°C/180°C fan/gas mark 6. Fill 8 holes of a 12-hole muffin tin with large muffin cases, or 12 cake cases if making the smaller version.
2 Beat the eggs in a large bowl. Sift in the flours, baking powder, salt and bicarbonate of soda. Pour in the milk and yoghurt and mix to combine.
3 Peel, core and coarsely grate the apple and fold into the mix along with the Cheddar, sun-dried tomatoes, oregano and melted butter.
4 Spoon into the muffin cases and bake for 20–25 minutes, until risen and golden.
5 Remove from the oven and leave to cool on a wire rack. Best eaten on the same day although they will keep for a couple of days stored in an airtight container.

VARIATIONS

This recipe is so versatile. Why not try other combinations, such as roasted pepper and goat's cheese, Cheddar and baby spinach, or for pizza in muffin form, sun-dried tomato, mozzarella and pesto?

BUCKWHEAT GALETTES WITH GRUYÈRE, HAM & APPLE

SERVES: 4 • PREP TIME: 15 MINUTES, PLUS RESTING (AT LEAST
2 HOURS, PREFERABLY OVERNIGHT) • COOK TIME: 25–30 MINUTES

Buckwheat galettes – *galettes de sarrasin* – are thin, crisp, crêpe-style
pancakes popularised in Lower Brittany, in France. The galette is
made with buckwheat flour, a little wheat flour (which must not exceed
30% of the total weight of flour), milk and eggs, and has a savoury filling
(typically, ham and cheese, cheese and tomato, ratatouille, or cheese
and spinach, and topped with an egg – known as a *galette complète*).
Once filled, the edges of the galette are folded in to create a square,
open envelope.

GALETTES
165g buckwheat flour
    (available in most health
    food stores)
65g plain flour
2 eggs
600ml milk
½ tsp salt
2 tbsp butter, plus extra
    for greasing

FILLING
2 medium well-flavoured dessert
    apples (try Epicure, George Cave
    or Tydeman's Early Worcester)
6 cooked ham slices, cut into
    small pieces
150g Gruyère cheese, coarsely
    grated
Freshly ground black pepper,
    to taste

1 First, make the batter: add the flours, eggs, milk and salt together
  in a large bowl and whisk until the mixture forms a smooth,
  thick batter. Refrigerate for at least 2 hours, preferably overnight.
  (There is some debate among cooks about how long to 'rest' the
  batter for. I find the galettes are more tender if the batter has been
  rested overnight.)

2 Preheat the oven to 200°C/180°C fan/gas mark 6.

3 Set a frying pan over a medium heat and rub a little butter around the pan using a piece of kitchen paper. Ladle on some batter (2 tablespoons is about right for a 20cm/8 inch frying pan). It's helpful to use a ladle, if you have one, so the batter can be poured into the hot pan in one go but don't worry if you haven't got one to hand, 2 tablespoonfuls of batter added in quick succession will do just fine. Cook the galette on one side until brown, 2–3 minutes, and then flip it over and cook for another minute or so. Remove from the pan and set aside.

4 To fill the galettes: wash, core and thinly slice the apples and place a few slices on each galette. Scatter over the ham and grated cheese and season with black pepper. Fold in the edges to make a square envelope and transfer to a large baking sheet. Melt a couple of tablespoons of butter and drizzle over the galettes.

5 Bake for 6–7 minutes, until crisp. Serve warm, on its own or with salad leaves.

NOTE

Buckwheat is a buff-coloured, gluten-free seed, distantly related to rhubarb and sorrel. It is nutrient-rich, higher in protein than other grains and is a good source of vitamin B. It has a strong, distinctive, slightly nutty flavour that works well in savoury dishes.

Spicy Tuna & Apple Wraps

SERVES: 2 • PREP TIME: 5 MINUTES

Ideal as a quick and easy lunch at home or to take to work, packed with flavour.

2 soft flour tortillas
2 tbsp hummus
1 × 120g tin tuna in sunflower oil
   or spring water, drained
2 tbsp mayonnaise
1 tsp garam masala

½ red onion, finely chopped
Sea salt and freshly ground
   black pepper, to taste
1 medium dessert apple (try
   Epicure, Laxton's Early
   Crimson or Lord Peckover)

1 Lay the tortillas on 2 serving plates and spread each with a tablespoon of hummus.
2 Flake the tuna into a small bowl and add the mayonnaise, garam masala and the red onion. Stir to thoroughly combine then season with salt and black pepper.
3 Spoon the tuna mixture down the centre of each of the tortillas, leaving a 2.5cm (1 inch) edge at either end.
4 Wash, core and thinly slice the apple and arrange the slices on top of the tuna.
5 Roll up the wraps, cut in half on the diagonal and serve immediately. Alternatively, wrap securely in cling film and enjoy as a tasty packed lunch.

Apple & Cheddar Scones

MAKES: 12 SMALL SCONES • PREP TIME: 10 MINUTES •
COOK TIME: 15 MINUTES

Serve spread with butter as a snack, as part of a ploughman's lunch or filled with chutney, cheese, ham or apple slices.

50g unsalted butter, chilled and diced, plus extra for greasing

250g self-raising flour, plus extra for dusting

Good pinch of salt

1 tsp baking powder

1 tsp English mustard powder

100g extra-mature Cheddar, coarsely grated

1 medium sweet dessert apple (try Laxton's Early Crimson, John Huggett, Morgan's Sweet or Zari®)

120ml milk, more if necessary

1 Preheat the oven to 200°C/180°C fan/gas mark 6. Grease and flour a large baking sheet.
2 Sift the flour, salt and baking powder into a large bowl. Rub in the butter using your fingertips, until the mixture resembles fine breadcrumbs. Then, stir in the mustard powder and half of the cheese.
3 Peel, core and coarsely grate the apple and fold into the flour.
4 Add the milk, a little at a time, and stir with a cutlery knife until the mixture forms a soft dough.
5 Turn the dough out onto a well-floured surface and roll out to about 2.5cm (1-inch) thick. Dip a 5cm (2-inch) round cutter in some flour and then use it to stamp out 12 rounds, re-rolling the dough as necessary. (Smooth-edged cutters tend to cut more cleanly, giving a better rise.)
6 Place on the baking sheet and sprinkle the tops with the remaining Cheddar.
7 Bake for 12–15 minutes, until risen and golden. Leave to cool on a wire rack. Best eaten just-warm on the same day.

Proscuitto, Apple & Burrata Tartlets

MAKES: 12 BITES • PREP TIME: 10 MINUTES • COOK TIME: 20–25 MINUTES

This dish was inspired by an appetiser my husband and I shared at a beautiful rooftop restaurant in Palermo. Whilst I can't promise you a Sicilian sunset in food form it still tastes pretty good.

2 medium dessert apples
    (try George Cave, Gladstone
    or Irish Peach)
Juice of ½ lemon
120ml cold water
Butter, for greasing
2 sheets of puff pastry

50g prosciutto crudo
150g burrata cheese
    (available from most
    Italian delicatessens),
    thinly sliced
1 egg, beaten
Sesame seeds, for sprinkling

1 First prepare the fruit. Peel, quarter, core and slice the apples (1.5cm/½-inch thick is ideal). Immediately toss in the lemon juice to prevent browning. Add the sliced apple to a large saucepan along with the water and bring to the boil. Reduce the heat, cover and simmer, stirring occasionally, until the apple is tender, 10–15 minutes. If the apple begins to stick to the bottom of the pan, add another tablespoon of water.

2 Remove the pan from the heat, drain and set aside to cool.

3 Preheat the oven to 200°C/180°C fan/gas mark 6 and grease a baking tray.

4 Slice the puff pastry sheet in half and place one half on the baking tray. Cover with the prosciutto, add the burrata cheese and then layer on the cooked apple.

5 Top with the second half of pastry and lightly brush with egg.

6 Sprinkle sesame seeds over the top.

7 Bake for 15 minutes, until the pastry is a light golden brown. Reduce the oven temperature to 170°C/150°C fan/gas mark 3 and continue to bake until the pastry is a deep golden brown. Serve warm.

Apple Focaccia with Provolone

MAKES: 1 FOCACCIA • PREP TIME: 30 MINUTES,
PLUS 2 HOURS' PROVING • COOK TIME: 20 MINUTES

This focaccia may not be one hundred per cent authentic but it tastes great. Ideal as a tear 'n' share bread and tasty enough to eat on its own as a snack.

FOCACCIA
325ml hand-hot water
1 scant tbsp fast-action dried yeast
½ tsp caster sugar
500g strong white bread flour
10g salt
4 tbsp extra-virgin olive oil,
    plus extra for greasing

TOPPING
Extra-virgin olive oil, to drizzle
Good pinch of flaky sea salt

2 sprigs of rosemary, leaves
    picked and chopped
1–2 medium sweet-sharp
    dessert apples (try
    Discovery, John Huggett
    or Tydeman's Early
    Worcester)
100g provolone piccante
    cheese (available from
    most Italian delicatessens)
    or young Asiago cheese,
    coarsely grated

1 Pour the hot water into a small bowl and sprinkle over the yeast and sugar. Stir to blend. Set aside for about 10 minutes, until the mixture is slightly foamy.

2 Add the flour and salt to a large bowl. Pour in the yeast mixture and add the olive oil. Mix until the dough clumps together.

3 Turn the dough out onto a clean surface and knead until it is smooth and elastic, about 10 minutes. Form the dough into a round.

4 Wipe the bowl clean and drop in the dough. Cover with cling film and place in a warm, draught-free area until the dough has doubled in size, about 1½ hours.

5 Lightly oil a shallow baking sheet.

6 Tip the dough onto a clean work surface and press into a rough rectangle. Transfer to the prepared baking sheet and press the dough into the tray, right into the corners. Cover with cling film and leave to rise for 30 minutes.

7 Preheat the oven to 220°C/200°C fan/gas mark 7.

8 When the dough is puffed, use your fingertips to poke deep holes across the surface, almost to the bottom. Drizzle generously with olive oil and sprinkle with sea salt and rosemary. Bake for 10 minutes.

9 Meanwhile, wash, core and slice the apple into 3mm (⅛-inch) thick rounds. Remove the focaccia from the oven and arrange the apple slices over the top.

10 Reduce the temperature to 180°C/160°C fan/gas mark 4 and return to the oven for 8 minutes.

11 Remove from the oven and scatter the cheese over the top. Bake for a further 2–3 minutes to allow the cheese to melt.

12 Remove from the oven and leave to cool on a wire rack for 10 minutes. Best served warm.

PORK & APPLE BURGERS WITH PICKLED RED CABBAGE

SERVES: 6 • PREP TIME: 20 MINUTES, PLUS I HOUR
CHILLING (OPTIONAL) • COOK TIME: 30 MINUTES

Use lean mince for healthy, hearty and flavoursome burgers. Serve
with tangy pickled red cabbage.

BURGERS

I firm dessert apple (try Gladstone
  or Tydeman's Early Worcester)
500g lean pork mince
55g breadcrumbs (see page 17)
I tsp dried oregano
I egg, lightly beaten
Salt and freshly ground black
  pepper, to taste
2 tbsp plain flour, for dusting
I tsp olive oil, for frying

PICKLED RED CABBAGE

2 tbsp red wine vinegar
I½ tbsp caster sugar
Salt and freshly ground black
  pepper, to taste
I small red onion, finely sliced
200g red cabbage, finely shredded
2 tsp wholegrain mustard

6 brioche burger buns, split in half,
  to serve

1 Peel, core and very finely chop the apple. Add all the ingredients for
   the burgers to a large bowl and season with salt and black pepper.
   Mix until well combined.
2 Divide the mixture into 6, roll into balls and flatten each into a nice,
   thick patty.
3 Add a little flour to a large plate. Dab each burger in the flour on both
   sides, then transfer to a baking tray. Cover with cling film and chill
   in the fridge for at least an hour. (Chilling the patties helps to prevent
   them falling apart during cooking but you can skip this step if you're
   in a hurry.)
4 While the burgers rest, make the pickled red cabbage. Stir the vinegar
   and caster sugar together in a bowl until the sugar has dissolved.
   Season well and stir in the onion, cabbage and wholegrain mustard.
   Set aside to soften while the burgers cook.

5 Preheat the oven to 190°C/170°C fan/gas mark 5. Line a baking sheet with foil.

6 Heat the olive oil in a frying pan until moderately hot. Add the burgers and fry for a minute on each side, until just browned. Remove from the pan and transfer to the prepared baking sheet.

7 Bake in the oven for 15 minutes, until cooked through.

8 Place a burger in each bun and top with pickled cabbage. Serve with your side(s) of choice.

Ensalada Paradiso

SERVES: 4, AS A SIDE • PREP TIME: 10 MINUTES

I saw a description of this intriguing-sounding salad in an article on *elrestaurante.com*. The original, served at Mercaderes restaurant in Mexico City, combines jicama – a crisp, slightly sweet root vegetable with white-coloured flesh common in Mexican and Asian cuisine – with apples, celery and strawberries on a bed of leaves.

Jicama is a little harder to find in the UK – although it is available in some Asian supermarkets – so I've substituted it with water chestnuts, which have a similar texture and flavour.

2 medium dessert apples (try
    Beauty of Bath or Epicure)
150g strawberries, hulled and sliced
2 celery sticks, trimmed and sliced
225g (140g drained) water chestnuts,
    rinsed, drained and sliced
½ head round lettuce, outer leaves
    removed and roughly chopped
½ head Romaine lettuce, outer
    leaves removed and roughly
    chopped

150g quesco fresco or mild feta
75g pistachios, roughly chopped

TAMARIND & HONEY VINAIGRETTE
2 tbsp tamarind paste
1½ tbsp clear, runny honey
3 tbsp rice vinegar
3 tbsp extra-virgin olive oil
Juice of 1 lime
Pinch of ground white pepper

1 First, make the vinaigrette. Add all the ingredients for the dressing to a small, screwtop jar and shake until the mixture has emulsified. Place in the fridge until needed.
2 Wash, quarter, core and thinly slice the apples, peel on. Add to a large bowl along with the strawberries, celery and water chestnuts. Remove the dressing from the fridge, shake again and then drizzle over the top of the fruit. Toss to coat.
3 Mix the chopped lettuce together in another large bowl and divide among four serving plates.
4 Spoon the apple mixture on top of the leaves and scatter with crumbled cheese and pistachios. Serve immediately.

Mexican Brown Rice Salad

SERVES: 4 • PREP TIME: 20 MINUTES • COOK TIME: 5–6 MINUTES

This zingy salad is packed with flavour and very satisfying. (See the photo for this recipe on page 40.)

SALAD

55g pine nuts
Olive oil, for drizzling
2 sweetcorn cobs
Salt and freshly ground
    black pepper, to taste
200g brown rice, cooked
1 × 215g tin red kidney beans,
    rinsed and drained
1 red pepper, deseeded and
    finely chopped
Small bunch of spring onions,
    finely chopped
Seeds from 1 pomegranate
1 medium dessert apple (try
    Discovery, Gladstone or
    Tydeman's Early Worcester)
Small bunch of coriander, chopped
150g queso fresco or mild feta
    cheese, crumbled

DRESSING

4 tbsp extra-virgin olive oil
3 tbsp white wine vinegar
Juice of 1 lime
1 shallot, minced
1 tsp ground cumin
1 garlic clove, minced

1 Preheat the oven to 180°C/160°C fan/gas mark 4. Spread the pine nuts out on a baking sheet and drizzle with a little olive oil. Bake for 5–6 minutes, until lightly toasted. Remove from the oven and set aside.
2 Meanwhile, heat the grill to medium and lay the corn cobs on a baking sheet. Brush with a little olive oil and season with salt and black pepper. Grill for 5–6 minutes, turning regularly, until the corn has a little colour. Allow to cool before removing the kernels from the cob.
3 To make the dressing, pour all the ingredients into a small, screwtop jar and season with salt and black pepper. Shake to combine, then set aside.
4 Add the brown rice, kidney beans, red pepper, spring onions, pomegranate seeds, toasted pine nuts and sweetcorn to a large bowl. Wash, core and finely chop the apple, peel on and then add to the rice mixture. Stir well to mix through.
5 Shake the dressing again and then drizzle over the rice salad. Stir the coriander through just before serving and top with the crumbled cheese.

WALDORF SALAD

SERVES: 4, AS A SIDE • PREP TIME: 5 MINUTES • COOK TIME: 20 MINUTES

This time-honoured classic was created for a charity ball held at the Waldorf-Astoria Hotel, New York, in 1896 and credited to the then maître d'hôtel, Oscar Tschirky. The original recipe was comprised of just apple, celery and mayonnaise with the walnuts being added later.

SALAD
150g seedless red grapes on
   the stalk
1 tbsp olive oil, for drizzling
Sea salt and freshly ground
   black pepper, to season
Handful of walnut halves
2 sweet-sharp dessert apples
   (try Discovery or Gladstone)
4 celery sticks, washed, trimmed
   and sliced into 1cm (½ inch) pieces
1 tbsp lemon juice
1 Romaine lettuce, outer
   leaves removed and
   roughly chopped

DRESSING
6 tbsp mayonnaise (or natural
   yoghurt sweetened with a
   dash of clear honey)
1 tsp English mustard
1 tbsp lemon juice

1 Heat the oven to 180°C/160°C fan/gas mark 4. Lay the grapes on a baking sheet. Drizzle with a little olive oil and season with sea salt and black pepper. Bake for 15 minutes. Add the walnuts to the baking sheet and cook for another 5–6 minutes, until the grapes are soft. Remove from the oven and set aside to cool.
2 Meanwhile, make the dressing. Add the mayonnaise and mustard to a small bowl and whisk. Stir in the lemon juice and season to taste.
3 Wash, core and thinly slice the apples, peel on, and add to a large bowl along with the celery. Immediately toss in the lemon juice to prevent browning.
4 Coarsely chop the toasted walnuts and add half to the bowl.
5 Remove the grapes from the stalk, add to the bowl along with the lettuce and toss well.
6 Divide among 4 serving plates. Drizzle the dressing over the salad and scatter the remaining walnuts over the top.

Mango Chutney

MAKES: 2 SMALL JARS • PREP TIME: 15 MINUTES PLUS
OVERNIGHT SALTING • COOK TIME: 30 MINUTES—1 HOUR

A tasty accompaniment to cold meats, cheese, crackers and, of course, any kind of curry.

4 large mangoes, peeled, stoned and sliced into small chunks
Good pinch of salt
2 large cooking apples, about 450g (try Bramley, Grenadier or Reverend W. Wilks)
1 onion, finely chopped
2 garlic cloves, minced

1 tbsp English mustard powder
1 tbsp fresh root ginger, peeled and minced
2 tsp cayenne pepper
½ tsp ground turmeric
400g caster sugar
375ml white wine vinegar

1 Add the mango to a large bowl and sprinkle with salt. Cover with cling film and leave in a cool place overnight. (The salt helps to reduce bitterness and therefore enhances the fruit's sweetness.)
2 In the morning, drain off the juice and rinse the salt off the fruit.
3 Peel, quarter, core and finely chop the apples. Add to a saucepan along with the onion, garlic, mustard, ginger, cayenne pepper, turmeric, sugar and vinegar. Cook over a low heat, stirring occasionally, until the sugar has dissolved.
4 Bring to the boil, then add the mango. Reduce the heat and simmer, uncovered, for 30 minutes, stirring frequently to make sure that it doesn't stick, until the mixture is thick and pulpy. Spoon into hot, sterilised jars (see page 31) and seal. *Leave to mature in a cool, dark place for at least 2 months before using.*

Apple & Raspberry Frangipane Cake

SERVES: 6 • PREP TIME: 15 MINUTES • COOK TIME: 1 HOUR 15 MINUTES

This moist, dense cake is so simple to make and very tasty. Why not try apple and apricot or apple and cherry too?

225g self-raising flour
Good pinch of salt
110g caster sugar
50g ground almonds
110g butter, diced
2 eggs, beaten

3 tbsp milk
3 medium dessert apples (try Beauty of Bath, Devonshire Quarrenden or Discovery)
150g raspberries
2 tbsp flaked almonds, for topping

1 Preheat the oven to 180°C/160°C fan/gas mark 4. Grease a 20cm (8 inch) loose-bottomed cake tin and line the base with baking parchment.
2 Sift the flour into a large bowl. Add the salt and stir in the caster sugar and ground almonds. Using your fingertips, rub in the butter until the mixture resembles fine breadcrumbs.
3 Add the egg and stir in the milk, 1 tablespoon at a time. Mix well to combine.
4 Peel, core and coarsely grate the apple and fold into the batter along with half of the raspberries.
5 Spoon the batter into the prepared cake tin and level out the top. Decorate with the remaining raspberries, 'planting' them lightly in the batter. Sprinkle the flaked almonds across the top.
6 Bake for 1 hour 15 minutes (cover with foil if the cake is beginning to brown too much), or until a skewer inserted in the middle of the cake comes out almost clean.
7 Allow the cake to cool in the tin for 10 minutes before turning out onto a wire rack to cool completely. Serve cold.

Apple & Raspberry Cobbler

SERVES: 4 • PREP TIME: 20 MINUTES • COOK TIME: 35–40 MINUTES

A fuss-free summer pudding with a scone-like topping.

2 tbsp butter, plus extra for greasing
500g dessert apples (try berry-like Devonshire Quarrenden or Worcester Pearmain)
100g raspberries
3 tbsp caster sugar

COBBLER TOPPING
350g self-raising flour, plus extra for dusting

Pinch of salt
Pinch of ground cinnamon
Pinch of ground ginger
150g butter, chilled, cut into cubes
65g caster sugar
1 egg
50ml milk
Demerara sugar, for sprinkling

Custard or vanilla ice cream, to serve

1 Preheat the oven to 180°C/160°C fan/gas mark 4. Grease a deep, 1.5–1.75 litre ovenproof dish with butter.
2 Peel, core and slice the apples and add to the prepared dish along with the raspberries. Sprinkle over the caster sugar and stir to mix. Dot with a few small pieces of butter.
3 To make the cobbler topping: sift the flour into a large bowl and stir in the salt, cinnamon and ginger. Using your fingertips, rub in the butter until the mixture resembles fine breadcrumbs, then stir in the caster sugar.
4 Add the egg and milk to a small bowl and stir to combine.
5 Slowly pour the egg mixture into the flour, reserving a little for brushing. Stir with a cutlery knife until the mixture comes together. Turn out onto a floured surface and knead lightly into a smooth dough.
6 Roll the dough out to 1.5cm (½-inch) thick and, use a 5.5cm (2 inch) pastry cutter to stamp out 12 rounds, re-rolling the dough if necessary. Arrange the rounds over the top of the fruit. Brush the tops with the reserved egg-milk mixture and sprinkle with Demerara sugar.
7 Bake for 35–40 minutes, until the cobbler topping is risen and golden. Serve warm with custard or cold with vanilla ice cream.

Apple Citrus Cake

MAKES: 12–16 SQUARES • PREP TIME: 15 MINUTES •
COOK TIME: 50–55 MINUTES

This light, zingy sponge is perfect for a summer picnic.

400g tart cooking apples (varieties that cook to a purée work well. Bramley is a safe bet but why not try Emneth Early, Grenadier, Keswick Codlin or Reverend W. Wilks?)
Zest and juice of 1 unwaxed lemon
Zest and juice of 1 clementine

175g unsalted butter, softened, plus extra for greasing
150g golden caster sugar
1 tsp Sicilian lemon extract
3 eggs
300g self-raising flour, sifted
1½ tsp baking powder
Demerara sugar, for sprinkling

1 Preheat the oven to 180°C/160°C fan/gas mark 4. Grease and line a square baking tin (about 23cm × 23cm/9 inches × 9 inches) with baking parchment.
2 Peel, quarter, core and thickly slice the apples into a medium bowl and immediately toss in the lemon and clementine juices to prevent browning. Set aside.
3 Add the butter, sugar and lemon extract to a large bowl and cream together until smooth. Add the eggs, one at a time, add the lemon and clementine zest and then fold in the flour and baking powder. Lastly, fold in the apple and mix to ensure the fruit is evenly dispersed.
4 Pour the mixture into the prepared baking tin and smooth out the top with the back of a wet tablespoon. Sprinkle with the Demerara sugar.
5 Bake for 50–55 minutes, until golden and springy to the touch and a skewer inserted into the middle comes out almost clean. Leave to cool in the tin for 10 minutes then turn out and remove the baking parchment. Cut into squares. *Store in an airtight container for up to 3 days.*

APPLE SNOW

SERVES: 4 • PREP TIME: 15 MINUTES, PLUS 1 HOUR CHILLING •
COOK TIME: 15 MINUTES

This old-fashioned dessert is deliciously light and refreshing and best of all it's wonderfully simple to whip up.

2 large cooking apples, about 500g (a tart variety that cooks to a pulp works best. Bramley is a safe bet, or try Emneth Early or Reverend W. Wilks)

Finely grated zest and juice of 1 unwaxed lemon

75g caster sugar

50ml water

2 egg whites, at room temperature

200ml double cream

Digestive or sweet oat biscuits, to serve (optional)

EQUIPMENT

Handheld electric whisk

1 Peel, quarter, core and roughly chop the apples. Add to a medium saucepan along with the lemon zest and juice, 50g of the sugar and the water and cover with a lid. Cook over a low heat, stirring occasionally, until the apples have broken down into a purée, about 15 minutes. Mash with a fork to remove any stubborn lumps, then set aside to cool.

2 Add the egg whites to a sparkling clean, medium glass bowl. (Traces of grease in the bowl will prevent the egg white expanding properly.) Using an electric whisk, whisk the egg white until it forms stiff peaks. (A handheld electric whisk really is the best tool for the job where meringue is concerned.) Add the remaining 25g sugar and whisk again until it forms soft peaks. Gently fold into the apple purée using a large metal spoon. (A thick wooden spoon will knock the air out and cause the mixture to collapse.)

3 Whip the cream in a large bowl until it just holds soft peaks and, again, using a large metal spoon, gently fold into the apple meringue.

4 Spoon into four glasses or sundae dishes and refrigerate for at least 1 hour. Serve on its own or with digestive or sweet oat biscuits.

$\mathcal{A}$PPLE, $\mathcal{C}$LEMENTINE & $\mathcal{L}$IME COMPOTE

SERVES: 4 • PREP TIME: 15 MINUTES • COOK TIME: 20–25 MINUTES

This fresh and zingy compote can be served hot or cold. Enjoy it swirled through yoghurt or oatmeal at breakfast, spread on toast or scones or spooned onto ice cream or crushed meringues for an instant dessert. It can also be used as a filling for sponge cakes, tarts and crumbles.

2 large cooking apples, about 500g (try Bramley or Emneth Early)
Finely grated zest and juice of 2 clementines (or 1 large orange)
Finely grated zest and juice of 1 unwaxed lime
2 tbsp caster sugar, plus extra to taste

1 Peel, quarter, core and thinly slice the apples and add to a medium saucepan along with all the citrus zest and juice. Immediately toss the apples in the juice to prevent browning. Then stir in the sugar.
2 Simmer over a medium heat, stirring occasionally but vigorously to prevent it catching on the bottom, until the apples have cooked to a tender but textured purée, 20–25 minutes. (If using as the filling for a sponge cake or mini fruit tarts, you may prefer to cook the fruit for a little longer and mash any remaining lumps with a fork to create a smooth purée.)
3 Check for sweetness and add a little extra sugar, if desired.

$\mathcal{A}$PPLE & $\mathcal{R}$ASPBERRY $\mathcal{S}$ORBET

SERVES: 4 • PREP TIME: 35–40 MINUTES •
CHILLING TIME: 20–25 MINUTES

A fresh, deliciously fruity frozen treat. This is an intensely-flavoured
sorbet so you only need one or two small scoops per person.

600g well-flavoured dessert apples
(try berry-flavoured Devonshire
Quarrenden or Discovery)
Juice of l lemon
200g raspberries (or other
berries such as blackberries
or strawberries), plus extra
for garnish

60g caster sugar
240ml cold water

Brandy snaps, to serve
(optional)

EQUIPMENT
Ice cream maker

1 Wash, core and chop the apples into small pieces, peel on, and
immediately toss in the lemon juice to prevent browning. Transfer to
the bowl of a food processor along with the raspberries and blend
until very smooth.
2 Place a fine-mesh sieve over a large bowl and press the fruit purée
through with the back of a spoon. Discard the pulp left behind in
the sieve.
3 Add the sugar and water and stir until the sugar has fully dissolved.
4 Transfer to the bowl of an ice cream maker and freeze according to
the manufacturer's instructions. If you don't have an ice cream maker
see *No ice cream maker? No worries* on page 36.
5 Best served immediately after churning for a meltingly soft texture
(after that, ice crystals begin to form and the sorbet becomes slightly
grainy). Serve with some fresh berries and a brandy snap, if you like.

NOTE
Apples are ideal for sorbets. Their high level of pectin acts as a natural
thickening agent, giving the sorbet a smooth, creamy texture.

Peruvian Crazy Water

SERVES: 6 (MAKES ABOUT 1½ LITRES) • PREP TIME: 10 MINUTES •
COOK TIME: 35–40 MINUTES, PLUS COOLING

This sweet nectar, commonly known as *Agua de Locos* (Crazy Man's Water) is very popular in Peru not only for its delicious, refreshing taste, but as a nutrient-rich elixir said to relax and calm the mind.

Delicious chilled as a thirst-quenching summer cooler or served warm as a comforting winter drink.

8–9 medium or 5–6 large apples, about 1kg (a tart, well-flavoured variety would work well. Try Emneth Early, Lady Hollendale or Reverend W. Wilks. Sweet or very subtly flavoured apples are best avoided)

2 cinnamon sticks
2 whole cloves
¼ tsp ground allspice
Juice of 1 lemon
2 litres water
100g granulated sugar, or more depending on taste

1 Peel, quarter, core and coarsely chop the apples. Place in a large heavy-based saucepan along with the spices, lemon juice and water. Bring to the boil then reduce the heat and simmer, part covered, for 35–40 minutes until the apple is very tender. Remove from the heat and scoop out the spices. Set aside to cool for a couple of minutes.
2 Pour the apple mixture into the bowl of a food processor and blend until very smooth. Strain into a large jug, discarding the remaining solids. Add the sugar, according to taste, and stir until completely dissolved.
3 Refrigerate until needed. Serve chilled, or warm in colder months.

APPLE RASPBERRY SPRITZER

SERVES: 2 • PREP TIME: 2 MINUTES • COOK TIME: 10–15 MINUTES,
PLUS CHILLING

Blend fresh apple juice, raspberries and Prosecco into a light, refreshing summer cocktail.

350ml apple juice (I use a blend
  of Cox's Orange Pippin and
  Bramley apple juice)
100g raspberries, plus extra
  for garnish

2 tsp granulated sugar
2 tsp lemon juice
200ml Prosecco or soda
  water
Ice cubes, to serve

1 Pour the apple juice into a medium saucepan and add the raspberries. Simmer over a medium heat for 10–15 minutes until the liquid has reduced in volume by about a third. Use a spoon to skim off any foam that forms on the surface.
2 Remove the pan from the heat and set aside to cool for a few minutes. Then pass the reduction through a sieve into a jug, pressing the raspberries gently with the back of a spoon. Discard any pulp left in the sieve and place the jug in the fridge to chill.
3 To serve, add a teaspoon of sugar, a teaspoon of lemon juice and 1–2 raspberries to each of the highball glasses. Add a couple of ice cubes and pour in the apple and raspberry reduction. Top with the Prosecco (or soda water) and stir to mix. Serve immediately.

APPLE & RASPBERRY SMOOTHIE

SERVES: 2 • PREP TIME: 5 MINUTES

Whizz up this delicious, nutritious smoothie in no time. The perfect way to jumpstart your day.

1 large apple (Bramley and Grenadier are both good choices. Or, for sweeter taste try Devonshire Quarrenden or Discovery)
75g raspberries

1 slice of pineapple (about 40g), peeled and cut into chunks
1 tbsp clear runny honey, or to taste
100ml semi-skimmed milk
75g fat-free natural yoghurt
10 ice cubes

1 Peel, core and coarsely chop the apples. Then add all the ingredients to the bowl of a food processor and blend until smooth. Pour into glasses and enjoy.

NOTE
Freezing the fruit in advance will help thicken the smoothie.

Apple & Mango Smoothie

Rustle up this tempting tropical treat in minutes.

2 medium well-flavoured dessert apples (try Devonshire Quarrenden or Discovery)
I large mango, peeled, stoned and sliced into small chunks
½ ripe banana, peeled and sliced
I slice pineapple (about 40g), peeled and cut into chunks

2 tbsp clear runny honey, or to taste
200ml semi-skimmed milk
150g fat-free natural yoghurt (or Greek-style yoghurt if you prefer a thick smoothie)
8 ice cubes

1 Peel, core and coarsely chop the apples. Then add all the ingredients to the bowl of a food processor and blend until smooth. Pour into glasses and serve.

APPLE MOJITO

SERVES: 2 • PREP TIME: 2 MINUTES • COOK TIME: 10–15 MINUTES, PLUS CHILLING

If you don't own a juicer, shop-bought pressed apple juice (not from concentrate) works just as well for this recipe.

350ml apple juice (I use a blend of Cox's Orange Pippin and Bramley apple juice)

10–12 mint leaves, plus extra for garnish

1 tbsp light brown soft sugar

80ml white rum (or soda water)

Juice of 1 lime, about 2 tbsp

Ice cubes, to serve

1 Pour the apple juice into a small saucepan. Simmer over a medium heat for 10–15 minutes until the liquid has reduced in volume by about a third. Use a spoon to skim off any foam that forms on the surface.

2 Remove the pan from the heat and set aside to cool for a few minutes. Pour reduction into a jug and place in the fridge to chill thoroughly.

3 To serve, muddle 5–6 mint leaves with 1½ teaspoons of light brown soft sugar in the bottom of each of the highball glasses. Pour in the apple juice reduction, white rum (or soda water) and lime juice. Stir and add a few ice cubes. Garnish with apple peel, a slice of apple, tossed in lime juice to prevent browning or a sprig of mint, if desired.

4 Serve immediately. Repeat.

Autumn

ROASTED BUTTERNUT SQUASH, APPLE & CHILLI SOUP

SERVES: 4 • PREP TIME: 20 MINUTES • COOK TIME: 1 HOUR 10 MINUTES

Sweet butternut teams well with the sweet-sharp flavour of apple, and the subtle hit of chilli from the oil is guaranteed to add warmth on the gloomiest autumnal day. (See the photo for this recipe on page 80.)

CHILLI OIL
6 tbsp extra-virgin olive oil
½ tsp dried chilli flakes
Pinch of paprika
½ garlic clove, minced

1kg butternut squash, deseeded
  and cut into thin wedges
6 garlic cloves, unpeeled and
  bashed
8–10 sage leaves

4 tbsp olive oil
2–3 medium well-flavoured
  apples, about 500g (try Gala,
  Limelight, Maclean's Favourite
  or Merton Prolific)
1 litre vegetable stock (see page 15)
Sea salt and freshly ground pepper,
  to taste

EQUIPMENT
Hand blender or blender

1 Preheat the oven to 190°C/170°C fan/gas mark 5.
2 First make the chilli oil. Add all the ingredients for the chilli oil to a small saucepan and cook over a medium-low heat for 4–5 minutes. (The oil should be just hot enough to infuse the flavours.) Set aside until needed.
3 Place the squash wedges in a roasting tray, skin side down. Scatter the bashed garlic over the squash. Drizzle the olive oil over the top and season well with salt and black pepper. Cook for 20 minutes, then crush the sage leaves in your hand, to release the flavour and toss these into the tray too. Cook for a further 20 minutes.
4 Peel, core and coarsely chop the apples. Then, remove the sage leaves from the roasting tray and add the apple. Return the tray to the oven for a further 20 minutes, until the squash and apple are both very tender.

5 Squeeze the roasted garlic cloves out of their skins and add to a large saucepan, discarding any burnt ones. Add the apples, then scrape the squash flesh from its skin and add this to the pan too, along with any juices from the tray. Pour in half of the stock and whizz with a hand blender or transfer to a blender until very smooth and creamy. Add more of the stock, a little at a time, until you achieve your desired consistency. Mixing well after each addition.

6 Warm the soup through over a medium heat and season to taste. Drizzle with the chilli oil just before serving.

Spiced Carrot & Apple Soup

SERVES: 4 • PREP TIME: 10 MINUTES • COOK TIME: 30–35 MINUTES

This gently spiced soup is perfect for a crisp autumn day.

2 tbsp butter
1 medium onion, coarsely chopped
1 tbsp olive oil
2 garlic cloves, minced
2 tsp finely grated fresh root ginger
4 medium carrots, peeled and
    coarsely chopped
1 medium dessert apple (honeyed
    Alkmene (Early Windsor)
    works well here or try Cox's
    Orange Pippin, D'Arcy Spice or
    Ribston Pippin)

1 litre vegetable (see page 15) or
    chicken stock
1 tsp honey
1 tsp ground sumac, plus extra
    to serve (optional)
1 tsp ground cumin
Sea salt and freshly ground
    black pepper, to taste
Crusty bread, to serve

EQUIPMENT
Hand blender or blender

1 Melt the butter in a large, heavy-based saucepan over a medium heat. Add the onion and cook gently for 5–6 minutes, stirring occasionally, until soft and translucent. Reduce the heat if the onion starts to brown. Season lightly with salt and black pepper.
2 Add the olive oil, garlic, ginger and carrots to the pan and cook for a couple more minutes, stirring occasionally.
3 Peel, core and coarsely chop the apple and add to the pan with the remaining ingredients. Cover and bring to the boil, then reduce the heat and simmer for 25 minutes, until the carrots and apple are very tender.
4 Remove from the heat. Transfer to a blender or whizz with a hand blender until smooth, then pass through a sieve into a large bowl. Check for seasoning. Garnish with a sprinkling of ground sumac, if you like, and serve with warm, crusty bread.

NOTE
Sumac is an attractive and versatile spice widely used in Middle Eastern and Mediterranean cooking. It has a tart, lemony flavour and adds a lovely pop of colour sprinkled over food before serving.

BRAISED RED CABBAGE WITH BRAMLEY APPLE

SERVES: 4 • PREP TIME: 15 MINUTES • COOK TIME: 1 HOUR 30 MINUTES

This classic combination is great with roast beef, pork or game or as a tasty accompaniment to simple sausage and mash.

1 large Bramley apple
125g butter
100g light brown soft sugar
100ml red wine vinegar or
  malt vinegar
2 cinnamon sticks
2 star anise
¼ tsp ground nutmeg

¼ tsp ground cloves
Good pinch of salt and freshly
  ground black pepper
1 small red cabbage, finely
  shredded
1 raw beetroot, peeled and
  coarsely grated

1 Preheat the oven to 200°C/180°C fan/gas mark 6.
2 Peel, quarter, core and finely chop the apple. Set aside.
3 Add the butter, sugar and vinegar to a casserole dish and stir over a medium heat until the sugar has dissolved.
4 Add the cinnamon, star anise, nutmeg and cloves and season well with salt and black pepper. Add the apple, cabbage and beetroot and toss to thoroughly coat. Cover and transfer the casserole to the oven.
5 Bake for 1½ hours, stirring every 30 minutes or so, until the cabbage is very tender and the liquid has reduced to a thick, shiny glaze. Remove the cinnamon sticks and star anise before serving. *Store, covered in cling film, in the fridge for up to a week.*

BIRCHER MUESLI

SERVES: 2 • PREP TIME: 30 MINUTES, PLUS SOAKING
(PREFERABLY OVERNIGHT)

Bircher muesli was developed in around 1900 by Swiss doctor and pioneer nutritionist, Maximilian Bircher-Benner.

Shortly after opening his first clinic, Bircher-Benner developed jaundice and claimed to have overcome it by consuming large quantities of fresh apples (an extraordinary assertion at a time before the benefits of a diet rich in fruit and vegetables were known). He began experimenting with the effect that raw foods have on the body and, as a result, developed *Birchermüesli* (from the Alemannic German *'mues'* meaning 'mush' or 'purée' and the diminutive *'li'* – literally, 'Bircher's little mush'). Thus was born a dish consisting of soaked oats, fruit and nuts which he began promoting for its health benefits.

50g oats (I prefer whole rolled oats
    for a chunkier texture)
2 tbsp chopped dried apricots, or
    dried fruit of your choice
100ml apple juice
Splash of milk
2 medium dessert apples (a Cox-
    style variety would work well.
    Try Captain Kidd, Chivers
    Delight, Meridian or Sunset)

Pinch of salt
2 tbsp low-fat natural yoghurt

TOPPINGS
2 tbsp chopped nuts of your
    choice (traditionally, almonds,
    hazelnuts or walnuts)
Handful of berries such as
    blueberries or blackberries
    (optional)

1 First, soak the oats and the dried fruits in the apple juice for at least 30 minutes, or overnight if possible. Once the oats have softened, stir in just enough milk to give the oats a loose, porridge-y consistency.

2 Wash, core and coarsely grate the apples with the peel on. Sprinkle the grated apple with a pinch of salt, to prevent browning, and divide among two serving bowls. Spoon the oats over the apple, top with a tablespoonful of yoghurt and sprinkle with chopped nuts and, if using, a few berries.

ᴀPPLE & ꜱTILTON ʙRUSCHETTA WITH ꟽALNUTS

SERVES: 4 • PREP TIME: 10 MINUTES • COOK TIME: 4–6 MINUTES

This easy dish is full of flavour. Serve as a starter or as a light snack.

1 medium tart dessert apple (try Oxford Conquest, Rosemary Russet or Suntan)
100g Stilton, crumbled
1 loaf crusty bread, preferably ciabatta or baguette

Extra-virgin olive oil, for brushing
2 tbsp walnut halves, coarsely chopped
½ tsp cayenne pepper
Freshly ground black pepper, to taste

1 Preheat the grill to medium and line the grill pan with foil. Position the grill rack 7.5–10cm (3–4 inches) from the heat source.
2 Wash, core and finely chop the apple. Add to a small bowl and crumble over the Stilton. Mix to combine.
3 Slice the bread diagonally into 12 thick slices. Brush lightly with olive oil and toast until light brown on both sides.
4 Spoon the apple and Stilton mixture onto the toasts. Scatter the walnuts over the top and sprinkle with cayenne pepper. Season with black pepper, to taste.
5 Return to the grill and toast for another minute or two, until the cheese has melted. Serve immediately.

Apple & Brie Pissaladière with Caramelized Onions

SERVES: 4 AS A MAIN, 12 AS AN APPETISER • PREP TIME: 15 MINUTES,
PLUS 3 HOURS 30 MINUTES PROVING • COOK TIME: 45–50 MINUTES

Pissaladière is a rustic, savoury tart from the south of France. It may look a lot like pizza but it is decidedly French. Its main distinguishing feature is the crust; unlike the crisp, thin, bread-like base of Italian pizza, pissaladière has a thick, flakey crust – somewhere between focaccia and shortcrust pastry. And, where the tomato reigns supreme on Italian pizza, this French dish is traditionally covered with a generous layer of caramelized onions and topped with anchovies and Niçoise olives – commonly laid out in a harlequin pattern.

Although the crust takes a little time to prepare, it's well worth the effort.

CRUST

220ml hand-hot water
1 tbsp fast-action dried yeast
1 tsp granulated sugar
325g plain flour, plus extra for
    dusting
1 tsp salt
3 tbsp extra-virgin olive oil

TOPPING

1 tbsp extra-virgin olive oil
2 large sweet onions, thinly sliced

¼ tsp salt
Pinch of grated nutmeg
1 medium sweet dessert apple
    (try Kidd's Orange Red, Laxton's
    Superb, Maclean's Favourite
    or Sanspareil)
200g Brie, thinly sliced
Freshly ground black pepper,
    to taste
1–2 tbsp balsamic vinegar
Handful of basil leaves,
    for garnish

continued

1 First, prepare the crust. Pour the hot water into a small bowl and
   sprinkle over the yeast and sugar. Stir to blend. Set aside for about
   10 minutes, until the mixture is slightly foamy.
2 Add the flour and salt to a large bowl. Pour in the yeast mixture
   and add 2 tablespoons of the olive oil. Mix until the dough clumps
   together and forms a smooth ball. If the dough is too sticky, add a
   little extra flour.
3 Turn the dough out onto a lightly floured surface and knead until the
   dough is smooth and elastic, about 3 minutes. Wipe the bowl clean
   and use the remaining tablespoon of olive oil to lightly grease. Drop
   the dough in the bowl and roll it around to coat. Cover with cling film
   and place in a warm, draught-free area until the dough has doubled
   in size, about 1½ hours. Punch the dough down, re-cover and let it rise
   again until almost doubled in size, about 1 hour.
4 Sprinkle a little flour onto a large baking sheet. On a lightly floured
   surface, roll the dough out into a rectangle about 5cm (2 inches) larger
   than the baking sheet. Lay the dough on the sheet and press the sides
   up to form a raised edge. Cover with a clean, dry tea towel and leave
   to rise until slightly puffed, about 1 hour.
5 Preheat the oven to 220°C/200°C fan/gas mark 7.
6 While the dough is proofing, prepare the topping. Heat a tablespoon of
   olive oil in a frying pan over a medium heat. Add the sliced onions and
   sprinkle with salt and nutmeg. Cover and cook, stirring occasionally,
   until the onion is golden brown and tender, about 15 minutes.
7 Spread the onions on the dough base and bake for 15 minutes. Quarter,
   core and thinly slice the apple, peel on. Remove the pissaladière
   from the oven, arrange the apple on top of the onions and scatter over
   the Brie.
8 Return to the oven and bake for a further 15–20 minutes, or until
   the crust is golden brown. Sprinkle with black pepper, a drizzle of
   balsamic vinegar and garnish with torn basil leaves. Serve as a light
   meal with a green salad or on its own as an appetiser.

MOROCCAN LAMB TAGINE WITH BUTTERNUT SQUASH & APPLE

SERVES: 4–6 • PREP TIME: 20 MINUTES •
COOK TIME: 2 HOURS 35 MINUTES

Tender butternut squash and sharp apple combine perfectly for a delicious twist on this classic North African dish. Serve on a bed of couscous or rice.

Pinch of saffron, crumbled
2 tbsp warm water
Ikg extra-lean leg of lamb, cubed
Olive oil, for frying
2 medium onions, finely chopped
4 garlic cloves, chopped
1.5cm (½-inch) piece fresh root
    ginger, peeled and finely grated
2 tsp ground cinnamon
2 tsp ground cumin
3 tsp ground turmeric
3 tsp paprika
8 cardamom pods

800ml chicken stock
Salt and freshly ground black pepper
300g butternut squash, peeled and
    cut into 2.5cm (I-inch) chunks
2 medium tart apples (a variety
    that keeps its shape when
    cooked works best. Try Galloway
    Pippin, Howgate Wonder or
    Scotch Bridget)
2 tbsp coriander leaves, roughly
    chopped

Couscous or rice, to serve

1 Sprinkle the saffron into a small cup and add the warm water. Set aside until needed.
2 Pat the meat dry on some kitchen paper. (This helps to prevent the lamb spitting when cooked.)
3 Heat 2 tablespoons of olive oil in a large ovenproof saucepan over a medium-high heat. Brown the lamb in batches, taking care not to overcrowd the pan. Set the cooked meat aside on a large plate and add the next batch, adding more oil as needed.

continued

4   Position the oven rack in the lower third of the oven and preheat to 170°C/150°C fan/gas mark 3.

5   Add the onions and garlic to the pan and cook for 2–3 minutes before adding the ginger and other spices. Stir to dislodge any meaty bits from the bottom of the pan.

6   Return the browned meat to the pan. Add the saffron and stir in 600ml of the stock. Season well with salt and black pepper.

7   Cover the pan and transfer to the oven. Bake for 2 hours, stirring every 30 minutes or so, until the lamb is very tender. If the tagine is simmering too vigorously, reduce the oven temperature.

8   Add the butternut squash and remaining stock to the pan. Stir, and return to the oven. Bake for 20 minutes, until the butternut squash is just tender.

9   Meanwhile, wash and core the apples and cut into 2.5cm (1-inch) chunks, peel on. Add the apple to the pan and return to the oven for a further 10 minutes, until the apples are tender.

10 Remove the pan from the oven. Stir in the coriander and check for seasoning. Serve with couscous or rice.

Pork & Apple Stew with Thyme Dumplings

SERVES: 4 • PREP TIME: 15 MINUTES • COOK TIME: 1 HOUR 35 MINUTES

A comforting, hearty casserole topped with fragrant herby dumplings.

1 tbsp olive oil
2 onions, sliced
3 celery sticks, washed, trimmed and thickly sliced
3 bay leaves
2 sprigs of thyme, leaves picked
500g lean pork loin, cut into chunks
4 garlic cloves, minced
2 tbsp plain flour
2 tsp English mustard powder
4 tbsp cider vinegar
700ml chicken stock
1 medium dessert apple (a variety that keeps its shape when cooked works best. Try Charles Ross or Lord Hindlip)
2 leeks, washed, trimmed and thickly sliced

3 medium carrots, peeled and thickly sliced
Salt and freshly ground black pepper
Mashed potato and a slice of bread and butter, to serve

DUMPLINGS
140g plain flour
1 tsp baking powder
1 tsp English mustard powder
2 sprigs of thyme, leaves picked
½ tsp dried rosemary
2 tbsp whole milk
4 tbsp cold water
2 tbsp olive oil, plus extra for drizzling
Salt and freshly ground black pepper

continued

1 Add the oil to an ovenproof saucepan and set over a medium heat. Add the onions, celery, bay and thyme and cook until tender, about 10 minutes. Add the pork and cook for a few minutes, until lightly coloured.

2 Add the garlic, flour and mustard, then stir in the vinegar and stock.

3 Peel and core the apple and cut into chunks. Add to the pan along with the leeks and carrots. Bring to the boil, then reduce the heat, cover, and simmer for 1 hour, until the vegetables are tender.

4 Preheat the oven to 200°C/180°C fan/gas mark 6.

5 To make the dumplings, add the flour, baking powder, mustard, thyme and rosemary to a large bowl and stir to combine.

6 Add the milk to a small jug. Dilute with water then stir in the oil.

7 Gradually add the wet mixture to the dry and stir to form a soft, sticky dough. Divide the dough into 8 and roll into balls.

8 Place the dumplings on top of the stew and drizzle each one with a little oil.

9 Bake in the oven for 20 minutes, until the dumplings are golden on top. Serve with mashed potato and a slice of bread and butter to mop up the last of the sauce.

WEST COUNTRY 'SQUAB' PIE

SERVES: 6–8 • PREP TIME: 50 MINUTES, INCLUDING
30 MINUTES CHILLING • COOK TIME: 1 HOUR 15 MINUTES

'Squab' – or pigeon – pie is a traditional dish from the south west of England, with particularly close links to Cornwall, Devon and Gloucestershire. Contrary to its name, the pie doesn't contain pigeon but is instead made with lamb or mutton mixed with apples and spices.

In Devon the custom is to serve squab pie with a dollop of clotted cream on the side. That's a tradition too far for me, but feel free to give it a whirl if you like!

PASTRY

225g plain flour, plus extra
    for dusting
Good pinch of salt
65g lard, cut into cubes
65g butter, cut into cubes,
    plus extra for greasing
1–2 tbsp cold water

1 egg, beaten with 2 tbsp water,
    for glazing

FILLING

1kg lamb neck, cut into cubes
1–2 tbsp plain flour, plus extra
    for dusting
Salt and freshly ground
    black pepper
2 tbsp vegetable oil, more
    if needed

2 leeks, trimmed, washed and
    thinly sliced
2 onions, coarsely chopped
¼ tsp ground cinnamon
¼ tsp grated nutmeg
½ tsp ground allspice
1 medium crisp dessert apple
    (for a touch of authenticity
    try a Cornish, Devonshire or
    Gloucestershire regional variety
    such as Ashmead's Kernel,
    Ben's Red, Cornish Aromatic
    or Duke of Devonshire)
1 large cooking apple, about
    200g (try Bramley, Tom Putt
    or Upton Pyne)
1 sprig of rosemary, leaves picked,
    finely chopped
2 bay leaves
500ml chicken stock

1 First, make the pastry. Sift the flour into a large bowl, add a good pinch of salt and, using your fingertips, rub in the lard until the mixture resembles fine breadcrumbs. Add the water, a little at a time, and knead lightly to form a ball of dough. Wrap with cling film and chill for at least 30 minutes.

2 Next, prepare the filling. Dredge the lamb in a little flour seasoned with salt and black pepper. This helps soak up excess moisture and prevents the meat spitting in the pan.

3 Heat 1 tablespoon of oil in a large saucepan and another tablespoon in a frying pan, so that you can brown two batches of meat at the same time. Cook the meat until browned on all sides, then transfer the lamb from the frying pan to the saucepan.

4 Add the leeks and onion to the frying pan and add a little extra oil, if needed. Cook over a medium heat until the onion is lightly coloured. Add to the saucepan along with the spices.

5 Wash, quarter, core and slice the apples, peel on (about 5mm/¼-inch thick is ideal). Add the apple to the lamb along with rosemary, bay and stock. Bring to the boil, then reduce the heat, cover, and simmer for 30 minutes, stirring occasionally. If the mixture starts to catch on the bottom of the pan, add a splash of water. (The mixture should be quite thick so don't add too much extra liquid, otherwise you could end up with a watery pie. No one wants that.)

6 Season with salt and black pepper and spoon the mixture into a greased ovenproof dish. Set aside to cool.

7 Preheat the oven to 200°C/180°C fan/gas mark 6.

8 Remove the dough from the fridge. Roll the pastry out on a lightly floured surface until large enough to cover the pie, with room to spare. Cut thin strips of pastry to line the edge of the dish and brush with water to moisten. Cover with the pastry lid and press down around the rim of the pie with a fork to seal. Trim off the excess pastry then re-roll your trimmings to make a decoration, if you wish.

9 Add the egg and water to a small bowl and whisk to make an egg wash. Brush heavily over the top of the pie, then use a small, sharp knife to make a couple of small cuts in the centre of the lid to act as vents.

10 Bake for 25–30 minutes, until the pastry is golden brown. Serve with seasonal vegetables and mashed potato.

Shropshire Fidget Pie

SERVES: 8–10 • PREP TIME: 45 MINUTES,
INCLUDING 30 MINUTES CHILLING •
COOK TIME: 50 MINUTES, PLUS 20 MINUTES COOLING

As a nation we have enjoyed Fidget Pie for more than 400 years but, like many heritage dishes, its precise origins are unclear. Shropshire has perhaps the strongest claim with the towns of Ludlow, Shrewsbury and Oswestry all responsible for their own variations. However, rival claims from other regions abound.

Similarly, no one really knows where the name 'Fidget' comes from. Some believe it is linked to the original five-sided shape, while others, rather sweetly, think it is named for the way the ingredients move around in the pastry case during cooking. My own personal favourite, though, arrives courtesy of the *Oxford English Dictionary*, which suggests 'fitchet-pie', as it was first called, is derived from 'fitchett', a dialect word for 'polecat', in reference to the strong odour that emanates from it during cooking. Whatever the truth, or truths, this filling, hearty pie tastes delicious.

Regardless of geography or etymology there is one common denominator: the basic ingredients remain the same. These include ham (usually gammon), apples and cider, cooked in a pastry case, sometimes with potato and onion. Traditionally Fidgets were made as a portable meal, carried in the pockets of farm workers – similar to a Cornish Pasty. These days, though, they are more commonly made as a large double-crust pie.

continued

PASTRY

450g plain flour, plus extra
  for dusting
Good pinch of salt
125g lard, cubed
150ml water
Butter, for greasing

1 egg, beaten with 2 tbsp water,
  for glazing

FILLING

2 large floury potatoes (such as
  Desiree, King Edward or Maris
  Piper), peeled and thickly sliced
2 medium onions, finely sliced
100ml double cream or crème
  fraîche

Salt and freshly ground
  black pepper, to season
1 large cooking apple (I prefer
  varieties that keep their
  shape when cooked such
  as Howgate Wonder and
  Scotch Bridget)
5–6 sage leaves, finely chopped
375g cooked thick-cut gammon,
  cut into 2.5cm (1-inch)
  chunks
1–2 tsp light brown soft sugar
100ml dry English cider (or
  1 tbsp cider vinegar mixed
  with 50ml apple juice and
  50ml water)
100g mature Cheddar cheese,
  coarsely grated

1 First, make the pastry. Sift the flour into a large bowl and add a
  good pinch of salt. Add the lard to a medium saucepan with 150ml
  water and set over a medium heat, until the lard has melted and
  the water is just simmering. Carefully pour the hot liquid into the
  flour and mix with a wooden spoon until it comes together. Tip the
  dough onto a well-floured surface and knead lightly to form a ball
  of dough. Wrap with cling film and chill for at least 30 minutes.
2 Preheat the oven to 200°C/180°C fan/gas mark 6. Line the base of a
  23cm (9 inch) deep loose-bottomed cake tin with baking parchment,
  grease the sides generously with butter and place on a baking sheet.
3 To make the filling, add the potatoes to a pan of lightly salted water.
  Simmer for 2–3 minutes, then add the onions and cook for a further
  2 minutes. Remove from the heat, drain well and pour in the double
  cream or crème fraîche. Season well with salt and black pepper, then
  set aside.

4 Remove the dough from the fridge. Roll two-thirds of the pastry out on a lightly floured surface to the thickness of a £1 coin and use it to line the bottom of the pie dish, leaving any overhang for the time being.

5 Peel, quarter, core and thickly slice the apple. Layer half of the apple into the pie case, followed by half of the potato and onion, sage and chopped gammon. Sprinkle with sugar and season well with salt and black pepper. Layer on the remaining apple, then the remaining potato and onion, sage and gammon. Carefully pour the cider over and top with the grated cheese.

6 Roll out the remaining pastry until large enough to cover the pie, with room to spare. Brush the rim of the pie shell with water and cover with the pastry lid. Press down all round the rim to seal. Trim off the excess pastry then re-roll your trimmings to make a decoration, if you wish.

7 Add the egg and water to a small bowl and whisk to make an egg wash. Brush heavily over the top of the pie, then use a small, sharp knife to make a couple of small cuts in the centre of the lid to act as vents.

8 Bake for 1 hour until golden. Turn off the heat and allow the pie to cool in the oven for 20 minutes. Serve cold in wedges.

PORK NORMANDY-STYLE

SERVES: 4 • PREP TIME: 20 MINUTES • COOK TIME: 3 HOURS

A classic combination of pork and apple, this slow-cooked hearty casserole is the ideal, warming comfort food for when the nights start drawing in. Perfect served with creamy mash and steamed cabbage.

2–3 tbsp olive oil
600g pork shoulder, fat and
    sinew trimmed, cut into
    2.5cm (1-inch) cubes
200g smoked bacon lardons
1 large onion, coarsely chopped
2 carrots, peeled and thickly sliced
2 celery sticks, thickly sliced
250ml dry English cider (or 2 tbsp
    cider vinegar mixed with 100ml
    apple juice and 100ml water)

2 medium firm apples (try
    Allington Pippin, Calville Blanc
    d'Hiver or King of the Pippins)
1 bay leaf
3 sprigs of thyme
1 chicken stock cube
400ml water
Salt and freshly ground black
    pepper, to taste
140g crème fraîche
2 tbsp Dijon mustard

1 Heat 1 tablespoon olive oil in a large saucepan over a medium heat. Brown the pork in batches, taking care not to overcrowd the pan, adding more oil as needed.
2 Add the lardons to the pan and cook until crispy. Set aside on a plate.
3 Add the onion, carrots and celery to the pan and cook until just tender, 5–10 minutes. Pour in the cider or apple juice and water, and simmer for a minute or two, scraping any meaty bits from the bottom of the pan.
4 Wash, core and chop the apples into 2.5cm (1-inch) dice. Add to the pan along with the herbs and crumble over the stock cube.
5 Return the pork and lardons to the pan. Stir in the water to dissolve the stock cube, and season well.
6 Reduce the heat to low, cover and cook for 2½ hours, stirring occasionally to prevent anything catching on the bottom of the pan. Check the casserole after about an hour or more, and if starts to look dry, add a splash of water.
7 Turn the heat up to high then stir in the crème fraîche and mustard. Cook for a further 5 minutes, stirring occasionally. Serve immediately.

BEETROOT, FETA & APPLE SALAD WITH PECANS

SERVES: 4, AS A SIDE SALAD • PREP TIME: 5 MINUTES •
COOK TIME: 5—6 MINUTES

Enjoy the flavours of autumn with this tasty side salad. For a light lunch add some shredded ham and serve with crusty bread.

80g pecans (or chestnuts,
    cooked and broken into
    bite-sized pieces)
2 medium crisp dessert apples
    (try Court of Wick, Edith
    Hopwood or Orange Goff)
2 medium beetroots (not in
    vinegar), peeled, quartered
    and thinly sliced
80g feta cheese, crumbled
Salt and freshly ground
    black pepper

DRESSING

1 tbsp red wine vinegar
3 tbsp extra-virgin olive oil,
    plus extra for toasting
½ tsp English mustard
Pinch of granulated sugar

1 Heat the oven to 180°C/160°C fan/gas mark 4. Spread the pecans out on a baking sheet and drizzle with a little olive oil. Bake for 5–6 minutes, until lightly toasted. Remove from the oven and set aside.
2 To make the dressing, pour all the ingredients into a small, screwtop jar. Shake to combine, then set aside.
3 Wash, quarter, core and thinly slice the apples, peel on, and add to a bowl. Add the beetroots and toasted pecans and crumble over the cheese. Shake the dressing again and pour over the salad. Lightly toss to coat and then arrange on four serving plates. Season with salt and black pepper before serving.

PEAR & APPLE TARTE TATIN

SERVES: 6 • PREP TIME: 5–10 MINUTES • COOK TIME: 25–35 MINUTES

Tarte Tatin is an upside-down pastry topped with caramelized fruit (traditionally apples), named after the Hôtel Tatin in Lamotte-Beuvron, France, where it is served as the signature dish.

There are a few other stories about the tarte's origins, the most common being that the dessert was the accidental creation of elderly sisters, Stéphanie (Fanny) and Caroline Tatin sometime in the 1880s. It is said that Stéphanie, who did most of the cooking in her family, set out to make an apple pie one day but inadvertently left the apples cooking in butter too long and, in a bid to salvage the situation, added a pastry base on top of the pan of apples and quickly finished the pie off in the oven. The dessert was a hit and by the time the sisters opened their hotel in 1894 the *tarte renversée des demoiselles Tatin* had quite a following.

It is worth noting that Sologne, the area surrounding the sister's hotel, was already known for an upside-down fruit tart, the '*tarte solognote*', so it is equally possible that the tarte Tatin was the sisters' own spin on a traditional, local recipe. Whatever the truth behind its creation, the tarte Tatin is now a classic and deservedly so.

Tarte Tatin was originally made with Reine de Reinettes (King of the Pippins) and Calville Blanc d'Hiver – both grown in the region – unpeeled with unsweetened flaky pastry and served warm on its own but, in my opinion, there's always a place for ice cream alongside.

Any Cox-style variety (such as: Alkmene (Early Windsor), Captain Kidd, Kidd's Orange Red, Meridian and Tydeman's Late Orange) would work wonderfully well. D'Arcy Spice, Egremont Russet and Lord Lambourne would also make excellent choices.

3-4 firm, well-flavoured dessert
  apples
2 large, firm pears
Juice of I lemon
120g unsalted butter, softened
  and cubed
200g caster sugar
250g puff pastry block, chilled

Vanilla ice cream or crème fraîche,
  to serve

EQUIPMENT

You will need a heavy-based
ovenproof frying pan with
straight sides about 20cm
(8 inches) in diameter.

1 Preheat the oven to 200°C/180°C fan/gas mark 6.
2 Peel and halve the fruit and remove the cores with a melon baller or
  teaspoon. Toss them in the lemon juice immediately to prevent browning.
3 Spread the butter over the bottom of a heavy-based ovenproof frying
  pan – using your fingers is best, if a little messy – then sprinkle the sugar
  evenly all over.
4 Arrange the fruit in the pan, cut side up. Alternate the apples and
  pears in a circle around the outside. Place half an apple in the centre
  of the circle and top with another half of apple to create a flower shape.
  Cut the remaining apple into quarters and squeeze them into any empty
  spaces, packing in as much fruit as you can (this will help give the tart
  the right density and make slicing easier).
5 Roll out the puff pastry to roughly the thickness of a £1 coin and cut a
  circle 1-2cm (½-1 inch) larger than the pan. Prick the pastry all over
  using a fork, then lay it on top of the fruit. Tuck the pastry down around
  the fruit inside of the pan.
6 Cook over a high heat for 5 minutes and then reduce to the temperature
  to medium and cook for another 10 minutes, or until the fruit mixture
  has turned a deep, golden brown.
7 Place the pan in the top part of the oven and cook for 10 minutes. Reduce
  the temperature to 180°C/160°C fan/gas mark 4 and bake for a further
  10-15 minutes, or until the pastry is puffed and golden.
8 Remove from the oven and leave to cool for 5 minutes. Run the blade of
  a sharp knife all the way around the edge of the pan to loosen the tart.
  Place a large plate over the pan and gently invert the pan onto the plate
  and lift the pan off.
9 Best served just warm, about an hour after cooking. Serve with vanilla
  ice cream or crème fraîche.

BLACKBERRY & APPLE CRUMBLE SLICE

SERVES: 9 • PREP TIME: 15–20 MINUTES •
COOK TIME: 35–40 MINUTES

This delicious update on the humble crumble combines a shortbread base with an apple and blackberry filling and a crunchy oat topping. The ideal antidote to a rainy autumn day.

FILLING
400g apple (any well-flavoured variety that keeps its shape when cooked would work. Try Dumelow's Seedling or Howgate Wonder or, if you prefer a sweeter flavour, Kidd's Orange Red or Tydeman's Late Orange)
200g blackberries
75g caster sugar

SHORTBREAD BASE
45g caster sugar
75g butter, softened, plus extra for greasing

150g plain flour
½ tsp baking powder
3 tbsp milk

CRUMBLE TOPPING
50g plain flour
50g whole rolled oats
50g almonds, coarsely chopped
50g granulated or Demerara sugar
Pinch of salt
½ tsp ground cinnamon
¼ tsp ground ginger
75g butter

continued

1 Preheat the oven to 170°C/150°C fan/gas mark 3 and grease a square baking tin (approximately 20cm × 20cm/8 inch × 8 inch).

2 First prepare the filling. Peel, quarter, core and slice the apples and cut the blackberries in half lengthways. Add the apples and blackberries to a medium saucepan along with the sugar. Cover and set over a low heat until the juice begins to come out of the fruit. Increase the heat a little and cook until the fruit is tender. Set aside to cool.

3 Next, make the shortbread base. Cream together the caster sugar and butter, then add the flour, baking powder and milk and blend until smooth. The mixture will be quite dry, like a thick paste. Spread over the bottom of the greased baking tin and even out the top with a palate knife. Bake in the oven for 10 minutes. Leave in the tin to cool.

4 Next, make the crumble topping by mixing all the dry ingredients (flour, oats, almonds, sugar, salt and spices) together in a bowl. Add the butter to a small saucepan and melt over a moderate heat. Pour over the dry mixture and stir to combine.

5 Spread the cooked fruit over the shortbread base and sprinkle the crumble mixture evenly over the top. Bake for 15–20 minutes, until light golden brown.

6 Serve warm with custard or vanilla ice cream.

OZARK PUDDING

SERVES: 6–8 • PREP TIME: 15 MINUTES • COOK TIME: 35–40 MINUTES

This nutty fruit torte is known to have been a particular favourite of former US President, Harry Truman.

Although, as its name suggests, the recipe in its current form almost certainly comes from the Ozarks region of Missouri, it bears a strong resemblance to *gateau aux noisettes* (cake with hazelnuts), which was brought to the New World by the French Huguenots who settled in Charleston, South Carolina. Hazelnuts were uncommon in the US at that time, so the more plentiful pecan was used, and by the time the dish reached Missouri, black walnuts were frequently the order of the day.

50g plain flour
2½ tsp baking powder
½ tsp salt
2 eggs
175g light brown soft sugar
1 tsp vanilla extract

150g apples (moderately sharp culinary varieties that keep their shape when cooked work well. Try Annie Elizabeth, Galloway Pippin or Howgate Wonder)
125g pecans or walnuts, chopped

1 Preheat the oven to 170°C/150°C fan/gas mark 3. Grease a deep 23cm (9 inch) baking tin.
2 Add the flour, baking powder and salt to a small bowl and stir to combine.
3 Add the eggs to a large bowl and whisk until light and frothy. Then add the sugar, a little at a time, and whisk until thick. Stir in the vanilla extract.
4 Peel, quarter, core and thinly slice the apple (about 1cm/½-inch thick is ideal) and fold into the egg mixture. Then stir in the nuts.
5 Add the flour mixture and stir well to combine.
6 Spoon the batter into the prepared baking tin and level out the top. The pudding may look a little unpromising at this stage but don't worry, the finished article tastes great.
7 Bake for 35–40 minutes, until bubbly around the edges and browned on top. Allow the pudding to cool in the tin for 10–15 minutes before turning out on to a serving plate. Serve warm or at room temperature with whipped cream.

DORSET APPLE TRAYBAKE

MAKES: 12 SQUARES • PREP TIME: 20 MINUTES •
COOK TIME: 50–55 MINUTES

Recipes for this homely fruitcake abound with Devon, Somerset, Yorkshire and Wales also having their own versions. But since Dorset has adopted apple cake as its official culinary symbol, the West Country variety seemed the way to go.

Dorset apple cake is usually made with sweet spices, including cinnamon, and local tradition dictates it should be served with a hearty dollop of clotted cream. Some recipes call for the addition of sultanas but I think it's perfect just the way it is.

400g well-flavoured apples (varieties that hold their shape when cooked work best. Try Ashmead's Kernel or Lord Hindlip. Or a Dorset variety such as sharp cooker, Buttery d'Or or sweet Melcombe Russet)

Juice of ½ lemon

175g butter, softened and cut into pieces

175g golden caster sugar

1 tsp vanilla extract

3 eggs

300g self-raising flour

Pinch of salt

1½ tsp baking powder

1 tsp ground cinnamon

2 tsp ground ginger

3 tbsp milk, more if needed

Demerara sugar, for sprinkling

Clotted cream, to serve

1 Preheat the oven to 180°C/160°C fan/gas mark 4. Grease and line a square baking tin (about 23cm × 23cm/9 inch × 9 inch) with baking parchment.

2 Peel, quarter, core and thinly slice the apples. Immediately toss in the lemon juice and set aside.

3 Cream the butter and caster sugar together in a large bowl until light and fluffy. Add the vanilla extract and eggs and mix to combine.

4 Mix the dry ingredients (flour, salt, baking powder and spices) together in a separate bowl. Gradually incorporate the dry mix with the wet, alternating each addition of the flour mixture with a tablespoon of milk. (This helps to avoid over-mixing.) Stir until smooth and lump-free.

5 Spread half the cake mixture into the prepared baking tin. (The batter will be very thick – it needs to be stiff in order to support the weight of the apples.) Arrange the apple slices on top of the mixture, reserving a few pieces for decoration.

6 Cover with the remaining batter, level out the top and decorate with the reserved apple. Sprinkle generously with Demerara sugar.

7 Bake for 50–55 minutes, until golden and springy to the touch and a skewer inserted into the middle comes out almost clean. Leave to cool in the tin for 10 minutes then turn out and remove the baking parchment. Cut into 12 squares. Serve on its own or the Dorset way, with a generous dollop of clotted cream. *Store in an airtight container for up to 3 days.*

Apple Charlotte

SERVES: 4 • PREP TIME: 30 MINUTES • COOK TIME: 40–50 MINUTES

A Charlotte is a moulded buttered-bread pudding with a puréed fruit (typically apple or pear) or custard filling.

As with a number of classic dishes, there is uncertainty surrounding the origin of the name 'charlotte'. Some believe it to be a corruption of the Old English *charlyt*, meaning 'dish of custard', while others say that it was named after Queen Charlotte, wife of King George III.

1kg apples (varieties that cook to a pulp work best. Try Arthur W. Barnes, Blenheim Orange or Bramley)
Finely grated zest of 1 orange plus 2 tbsp of juice

175g butter
120g caster sugar
12 slices white bread, crusts removed

Custard, to serve

1 Preheat the oven to 200°C/180°C fan/gas mark 6. Peel, core and roughly chop the apples and immediately toss in the orange juice.
2 Add 25g of the butter to a large saucepan and melt over a medium heat. Add the chopped apple and orange zest, then stir in the sugar. Reduce the heat, cover, and cook for 10 minutes, stirring occasionally.
3 After 10 minutes, remove the lid and cook uncovered for a further 5–10 minutes, until the apples have broken down to a textured purée. Set aside to cool.
4 Melt the remaining butter in a pan. Cut the slices of bread in half, and then half again to make thin strips. Dip each strip into the melted butter and use to line a large mould, or ovenproof bowl. Use a pastry cutter to stamp out a round for the base.
5 Once the mould is lined, spoon in the apple purée. Top with another round of bread dipped in melted butter.
6 Bake for 30 minutes, until golden brown and crispy on top.
7 Remove from the oven and allow to cool in the mould for a few minutes before carefully turning out onto a warm serving plate. Serve straight away with custard.

WEST COUNTRY APPLE DAPPY

SERVES: 7 • PREP TIME: 15 MINUTES • COOK TIME: 30 MINUTES

A simple, scrumptious British classic of sweet, Swiss roll-style pastry filled with apple and cut into rounds.

2 medium dessert apples
   (why not try a West Country
   variety such as Ben's Red,
   Cornish Aromatic, Lucombe's
   Pine or Oaken Pin?)
1 tbsp lemon juice
1 sprig of rosemary
200g self-raising flour
½ tsp salt

50g butter, chilled, plus extra
   for greasing
2 tbsp caster sugar
2 tbsp clotted cream, plus extra
   for serving
110ml milk
Granulated sugar, for sprinkling

Clotted cream, to serve

1 Peel, quarter, core and finely dice the apples. Add to a small saucepan along with the lemon juice, rosemary and 2 tablespoons of cold water. Cover the pan, set over a medium heat and simmer for 5 minutes, stirring occasionally. Drain well and remove the rosemary. Set aside to cool completely.

2 Preheat the oven to 200°C/180°C fan/gas mark 6. Generously grease a 20cm (8 inch) loose-bottomed cake tin with butter and line the base with baking parchment.

3 Sift the flour into a large bowl and add the salt. Use your fingertips to rub in the butter until the mixture resembles fine breadcrumbs. Stir in the caster sugar and clotted cream, then add the milk, a little at a time, until the mixture forms a soft, slightly sticky dough.

4 Turn the dough out onto a lightly floured surface. Roll out into a rectangle roughly the same size as a piece of A4 paper. (The dough will be very soft so you may find it easier to roll it out on a piece of secured baking parchment.) Spoon the cooled apple mixture evenly over the dough.

5 Starting from the longer edge, roll up the pastry like a Swiss roll. Using a sharp knife, cut the pastry roll into 7 thick slices.

6 Place each pastry swirl, cut side up, in the prepared tin, arranging them in a circle with 1 in the centre – spacing them out as much as possible. Sprinkle some granulated sugar generously over the top.

7 Bake for 25 minutes, until golden. Remove from the oven and leave to cool in the tin for 10 minutes before turning out. Serve warm or cold with a generous dollop of clotted cream.

ℋOMEMADE 𝒜PPLE 'ℕEWTONS'

MAKES: 16 BISCUITS • PREP TIME: 15 MINUTES,
PLUS 1 HOUR CHILLING • COOK TIME: 25–30 MINUTES

A delicious, and addictive, take on the retro classic, fig roll, with soft,
buttery pastry wrapped around a sweet, apple and cinnamon filling.

PASTRY

200g plain flour, plus extra
    for dusting
Good pinch of salt
100g butter, cut into cubes
100g granulated sugar
1 egg
1 tbsp milk
¼ tsp vanilla extract

FILLING

2 medium well-flavoured apples
    (try Ashmead's Kernel or
    Howgate Wonder)
1½ tbsp butter
2 tbsp dark brown soft sugar
½ tsp ground cinnamon, plus extra
    for sprinkling
granulated sugar, for sprinkling

1 First, make the pastry. Add the flour to a medium bowl and stir in
   the salt.
2 In a separate bowl, cream together the butter and granulated sugar.
   Add the egg, milk and vanilla extract and combine until smooth.
   Pour in the flour mixture and stir. When almost combined, turn out
   onto a well-floured surface and knead lightly to form a soft ball of
   dough – a few presses is all you need. Wrap tightly in cling film and
   refrigerate for at least an hour.
3 Next, prepare the filling. Peel, quarter, core and very finely chop
   the apples. Add the butter to a medium saucepan and melt over a
   medium-low heat. Add the apple and stir in the dark brown soft sugar
   and cinnamon. Cook, uncovered, for 5 minutes, then cover and cook
   for a further 5 minutes, stirring occasionally. Remove from the heat
   and mash lightly with a fork but don't go too overboard, the pieces of
   apple should remain almost whole. Set aside to cool completely.

continued

4 Preheat the oven to 180°C/160°C fan/gas mark 4. Line a large baking sheet with baking parchment.

5 Remove the dough from the fridge and roll out on a well-floured surface to a rectangle, the same size as a piece of A4 paper. (The dough will be very soft and buttery so you may find it easier to roll it out on a piece of secured baking parchment and, once the filling has been added, transfer the baking parchment directly to the baking sheet.)

6 Cut in half lengthways, so that you have two long pastry strips. Spoon half of the filling down one side of each pastry strip, leaving a thin border down the edge. Brush the edges lightly with water and fold the pastry over into a log to seal. Gently press down to flatten slightly and then prick along the tops with a fork.

7 Place the logs, seal side down, on the baking sheet, about 5cm (2 inches) apart. (Even after chilling, the dough is prone to spreading.) Sprinkle with sugar and a little cinnamon.

8 Bake for 20 minutes, or until light golden brown. Remove from the oven and cool for 5 minutes before slicing each roll into 8 pieces. *Store in an airtight container lined top and bottom with kitchen paper for up to 7 days.*

Spiced Apple Muffins

MAKES: 10 SMALL MUFFINS • PREP TIME: 15 MINUTES •
COOK TIME: 15 MINUTES

Apples are ideal for muffins, adding both moisture and aroma.

50g baking block (such as Stork), cubed

50g caster sugar

1 large egg

100g self-raising flour

1 tsp baking powder

½ tsp ground cinnamon, plus extra for sprinkling

½ tsp grated nutmeg, plus extra for sprinkling

½ tsp salt

1 tbsp milk

100g tart apple (try Dumelow's Seedling, Howgate Wonder or Lane's Prince Albert)

granulated sugar, for sprinkling

1 Preheat the oven to 200°C/180°C fan/gas mark 6. Line a 12-hole muffin tin with paper cases.
2 Cream together the baking block and caster sugar in a large bowl, until light and fluffy. Add the egg and mix until smooth.
3 Sift the flour, baking powder, cinnamon and nutmeg into the bowl and add the milk. Stir well to combine.
4 Peel, core and coarsely grate the apple and fold it into the mixture.
5 Spoon the batter into the paper cases until three-quarters full. Mix the granulated sugar with a pinch each of cinnamon and nutmeg and sprinkle over the top.
6 Bake for 15 minutes, until well risen and golden. Leave to cool in the tin for 10 minutes before transferring on to a wire rack to cool completely. Store in an airtight container lined top and bottom with kitchen paper for up to 4 days. The kitchen paper helps to keep the muffins moist while preventing them becoming soggy.

VARIATION

For a delicious autumnal twist, try substituting half of the apple with an equal weight of blackberries.

Apple Crisps

A tasty and healthy alternative to snacking on potato crisps.

2 crisp, well-flavoured dessert
apples (Try Barnack Beauty or
Tydeman's Late Orange)
½ tsp ground cinnamon

EQUIPMENT
Mandolin

1 Preheat the oven to 140°C/120°C fan/gas mark 1. Line a baking tray with baking parchment.
2 Wash and thinly slice the apple through the core – a mandolin is best for this, if you have one, to get 1–2mm ($\frac{1}{16}$ inch) slices. Arrange in a single layer on the baking sheet and dust with cinnamon.
3 Bake for 45 minutes–1 hour, turning halfway through, and removing any crisps that have turned brown. Continue cooking until the apples have dried out and are a light golden brown. *Cool and store in an airtight container.*

APPLE & BLACKBERRY ICE CREAM

SERVES: 6–8 • PREP TIME: 20 MINUTES • CHILLING TIME: 20–25 MINUTES

Sometimes only ice cream will do, regardless of the temperature outside.

500g sweet, well-flavoured
    dessert apples (try Chivers
    Delight, Sanspareil, William
    Crump or Winter Gem)
Juice of ½ lemon
300g blackberries

ICE CREAM BASE
2 eggs
150g caster sugar
480ml double cream
240ml whole milk
160g Apple Cider Jelly (see opposite)

EQUIPMENT
Ice cream maker

1 Wash, core and chop the apples into small pieces, peel on, and toss in the lemon juice, to prevent browning. Transfer to the bowl of a food processor along with the blackberries and blend until smooth.
2 Tip the fruit purée into a medium bowl and place in the fridge. (If you prefer a silky smooth texture, pass the fruit purée through a fine-mesh sieve and press through with the back of a spoon to remove the seeds and any remaining lumps. Discard the pulp left behind in the sieve.)
3 Next, prepare the ice cream base. In a medium bowl, whisk the eggs until light and frothy, about 2 minutes. Add the sugar, a little at a time, and continue mixing until combined. Pour in the cream and milk and whisk until completely blended. Then add the apple jelly and beat until smooth. (If your jelly has set a little on the hard side, simply pass the ice cream base through a sieve to remove any extraneous lumps.)
4 Transfer the base to an ice cream maker and freeze following the manufacturer's instructions. Allow it to stiffen (about 2 minutes before it's ready) before adding the chilled fruit purée to the mix. Continue freezing for another couple of minutes before transferring to a freezer-proof container. If you don't have an ice cream maker see *No ice cream maker? No worries* on page 36.
5 Serve on its own or as a delicious accompaniment to apple pie or crumble.

Apple Cider Jelly

MAKES: ABOUT 900G • COOK TIME: 20–25 MINUTES

Henry VIII is said to have been rather partial to a spot of cider jelly, which may go some way to explaining his rather corpulent form in later life. This concentrated jelly is super-sweet but so tasty spread on toast or as an accompaniment to cheese and crackers.

600ml sparkling dry English cider
400g preserving sugar (jam sugar helps the jelly set
    more firmly but granulated sugar is fine too)
Good pinch of ground cinnamon

1 Place a white side plate in the fridge for testing the setting point.
2 Pour the cider into a medium saucepan and stir in the sugar and cinnamon.
3 Warm the pan over a low heat to dissolve the sugar, stirring constantly. Once the sugar has fully dissolved, increase the heat and bring to the boil. Boil rapidly for 15 minutes, until you see a rolling boil. Skim off any foam that comes to the surface with a spoon.
4 Test for the setting point by using the wrinkle test: remove the side plate from the fridge and spoon on a small amount of the boiling liquid. Return the plate to the fridge for 2 minutes, then check the surface of the jelly for any slight wrinkling. If there isn't any wrinkling, take another spoonful of liquid from the pan and place the plate back in the fridge for a further 2 minutes. As soon as some wrinkling appears, remove the pan from the heat.
5 Allow the jelly to cool for 5–10 minutes before pouring into hot, sterilised jars (see page 31). Add the lids and leave to cool to room temperature, without moving (otherwise the 'set' may be broken and you could end up with runny jelly). *Store in a cool, dry place for up to 2 years. Once opened, store in the fridge.*

Winter

Thai-inspired Pea & Apple Noodle Soup

SERVES: 4 • PREP TIME: 20 MINUTES • COOK TIME: 25–30 MINUTES

A wonderfully warming winter soup, with fragrant spices and a kick of heat.

300g tart cooking apples (try Cottenham Seedling, Edward VII or Northern Greening)
Juice of ½ lime
2 tbsp olive oil
2 tbsp Thai green curry paste, or to taste
1 garlic clove, minced
400g peas, fresh or frozen
1 litre vegetable stock (see page 15)

150g straight-to-wok noodles
Sea salt and freshly ground black pepper, to taste
Small handful of coriander leaves, finely chopped, to garnish
1 red chilli, deseeded and finely chopped, to garnish (optional)

EQUIPMENT
Hand blender or blender

1 Peel, core and coarsely chop the apples, tip into a bowl and immediately toss in the lime juice to prevent browning.
2 Heat the oil in a large, heavy-based saucepan over a medium heat. Add the Thai green curry paste, garlic, peas and chopped apple and sauté for a minute or two, until aromatic.
3 Pour in the stock. Cover the pan and bring to the boil, then reduce to a simmer. Cook for 20–25 minutes, until the apples and peas are very tender.
4 Remove from the heat. Whizz with a hand blender or transfer to a blender until smooth.
5 Cook the soup in the pan over a medium-low heat. Season with salt and black pepper, then stir in the noodles to warm through.
6 Serve garnished with coriander and finely chopped chilli, if using.

CREAMY APPLE & PARSNIP SOUP WITH PARSNIP CRISPS

SERVES: 4 • PREP TIME: 10 MINUTES • COOK TIME: 40–45 MINUTES

This lovely creamy soup is really satisfying – the perfect antidote for a cold winter's day. The sweetness of the parsnip combines wonderfully with the sharpness of the apple.

Groundnut oil adds extra depth of flavour and gives off a delicious aroma as you cook, but if you don't have it to hand, sunflower oil works fine as a substitute.

PARSNIP CRISPS
1 medium parsnip
6 tbsp groundnut oil
Salt, to taste

SOUP
1 tbsp butter
1 tbsp groundnut oil
2 medium onions, coarsely chopped
4 medium parsnips, peeled and sliced into 2.5cm (1-inch) pieces

3 large cooking apples, about 700g (try Ashmead's Kernel, Bramley or Lane's Prince Albert)
2 garlic cloves, finely chopped
1 tsp ground cumin
1 litre vegetable stock (see page 15)
125ml milk
Sea salt and freshly ground black pepper, to taste

EQUIPMENT
Hand blender or blender

1 To make the parsnip crisps, peel and slice the parsnip into rounds, as thinly as you can. Heat the groundnut oil in a frying pan until it is very hot. Fry the parsnip rounds in small batches, turning regularly, until they are golden brown. Remove from the pan with a slotted spoon and spread them out on a piece of kitchen paper to drain. Season with salt and set aside.

2 For the soup, melt the butter and oil in a large, heavy-based saucepan over a medium heat. Add the onions and parsnips and cook gently for 10 minutes, stirring occasionally, until the onion is soft and translucent. Reduce the heat if the onion starts to brown.

3 Meanwhile, peel, core and coarsely chop the apples. Add to the pan along with the garlic and cumin and cook for 2–3 minutes, stirring regularly. Season lightly with salt and black pepper.

4 Pour in the stock. Cover the pan and bring to the boil, then reduce to a simmer. Cook for 25 minutes, until the parsnip and apple are very tender.

5 Remove from the heat. Whizz with a hand blender or transfer to a blender until smooth, then pass through a sieve into a large bowl.

6 Stir in the milk and check for seasoning. Garnish with parsnip crisps just before serving.

TIP

The parsnip crisps can be made in advance – they'll stay crisp for an hour or two after cooking.

Spiced Peanut & Apple Tartlets

MAKES: 9 MINI TARTLETS • PREP TIME: 10 MINUTES • COOK TIME: 20 MINUTESS

Apples and peanuts make a fantastic combination. These tasty little pastries are simple to make and so moreish.

I sheet ready rolled puff pastry
Flour, for dusting

Juice of ½ lime
2 tbsp plain flour

PEANUT SAUCE
I tbsp toasted sesame oil
I tbsp rice vinegar
I tsp soy sauce
3 tbsp crunchy peanut butter
I tbsp light brown soft sugar
½ tsp cayenne pepper
80ml coconut milk
I garlic clove, minced

FILLING
I medium sweet dessert apple
   (try Barnack Beauty, Cornish
   Gilliflower or Roundway
   Magnum Bonum)
50g salted roasted peanuts,
   coarsely chopped
2 tbsp butter, melted, plus extra
   for greasing

1 Preheat the oven to 200°C/180°C fan/gas mark 6. Lightly grease a deep 12-hole muffin tin.
2 Lay the puff pastry out on a lightly floured surface and cut into nine equal squares. Use them to line nine holes in the muffin tin.
3 To make the peanut sauce, add all the ingredients to a screwtop jar. Shake vigorously until the peanut butter is well blended. Place a tablespoonful of sauce in the centre of each pastry case.
4 Wash, quarter, core and thinly slice the apple, peel on. Top each of the tartlets with 2–3 pieces of apple and sprinkle with the peanuts.
5 Lightly brush the pastry with melted butter. Bake for 15 minutes, until the pastry is a light golden colour. Reduce the temperature to 180°C/160°C fan/gas mark 4 and bake for a further 5 minutes, until the pastry is a deep golden brown. Allow the tartlets to cool for a few minutes, then get stuck in!

STICKY APPLE, SAUSAGE & BACON BAKE

SERVES: 4 • PREP TIME: 15 MINUTES • COOK TIME: 35 MINUTES

This warming, one-tray wonder is sure to be a family favourite.

500g baby potatoes
1 red onion, coarsely chopped
2 garlic cloves, finely chopped
2 sprigs of rosemary, leaves picked
2 tbsp olive oil
Sea salt and freshly ground
    black pepper
8 rashers smoked streaky bacon
8 good-quality pork sausages

1 medium dessert apple (a well-
    flavoured variety that keeps its
    shape when cooked works best.
    Try Ashmead's Kernel, Cox's
    Orange Pippin or Jonagold)

GLAZE
3 tbsp clear runny honey
3 tbsp wholegrain mustard

1 Preheat the oven to 180°C/160°C fan/gas mark 4.
2 Place the potatoes in a pan of water and boil for 5 minutes. Remove from the heat, drain well and slice in half.
3 Tip the potatoes into a large ovenproof dish. Add the onion and garlic and sprinkle over the rosemary. Drizzle with the olive oil, season well with sea salt and black pepper and toss to coat.
4 Wrap a piece of bacon around each sausage and add to the dish.
5 Place in the oven and bake for 20 minutes.
6 Meanwhile, wash and core the apple and cut into thick wedges. To make the glaze, add the honey and mustard to a small bowl. Stir to combine and season well.
7 Remove the dish from the oven. Toss in the apple wedges and drizzle the honey-mustard glaze over the top.
8 Return the dish to the oven and bake for a further 10 minutes, until the sausages are cooked through and the apples are tender.

Home-Style Chicken Curry

SERVES: 4 • PREP TIME: 20 MINUTES • COOK TIME: 35 MINUTES

A fragrant, flavoursome curry packed with aromatic spice.

2 onions, roughly chopped
6 garlic cloves, coarsely chopped
5cm (2-inch) piece fresh root ginger, peeled and coarsely chopped
1 medium apple (a variety that keeps its shape when cooked works best. Try Braeburn, Lord Hindlip or Sanspareil)
4 tbsp vegetable oil
2 tsp cumin seeds
1 tsp fennel seeds
1 tsp chilli flakes

1 cinnamon stick
2 bay leaves
1 tsp garam masala
1 tsp turmeric
1 green pepper, deseeded and coarsely chopped
600ml chicken stock
1kg cooked chicken, cut into 2.5cm (1-inch) chunks

Indian flatbreads or basmati rice, to serve

1 Transfer the onions to the bowl of a food processor and add 3 tablespoons of water. Blend to make a slack paste. Tip into a small bowl and set aside.
2 Add the garlic and ginger to the bowl of the food processor and add 4 tablespoons of water. Blend until smooth and then tip into a separate small bowl.
3 Wash, quarter, core and coarsely chop the apple. Set aside.
4 Add the oil to a large heavy-based saucepan and set over a medium heat. Combine the cumin, fennel, chilli, cinnamon and bay leaves and add to the pan in one go. Cook for a minute or so, until aromatic.
5 Add the onion paste to the pan and fry until the water has evaporated and the onion has turned a dark golden brown, 7–8 minutes. Add the garlic and ginger paste and cook for a further 2 minutes, stirring constantly.
6 Stir in the garam masala and turmeric and cook for 30 seconds before adding the chopped apple, green pepper and stock. Cook, uncovered, for 10 minutes.
7 Add the chicken and stir to coat in the sauce. Simmer for 15 minutes, until the masala has reduced to a thick sauce. Serve with warm Indian flatbreads or basmati rice.

BEEF & APPLE PIE

SERVES: 6 • PREP TIME: 20 MINUTES, PLUS 30 MINUTES CHILLING •
COOK TIME: 2 HOURS

The apple in this satisfying single-crust pie adds a wonderful hint
of sweetness.

FILLING
450g lean beef casserole
    steak, diced
2 tbsp plain flour
I tsp dried thyme
½ tsp ground cinnamon
¼ tsp garam masala
½ tsp ground ginger
½ tsp ground mace
Salt and freshly ground
    black pepper
Olive oil, for frying
I large onion, finely sliced
I large carrot, peeled and
    thinly sliced
187ml red wine

225ml beef stock
I medium apple (try Ashmead's
    Kernel, Cox's Orange Pippin
    or Tydeman's Late Orange)

PASTRY
200g plain flour, plus extra
    for dusting
Pinch of salt
75g lard
4 tbsp cold water, more if needed

I egg, beaten with 2 tbsp water,
    for glazing

Mashed potato, to serve

1 First, prepare the filling. Pat the meat dry on some kitchen paper to
   remove any excess liquid.
2 Add the flour, dried thyme, cinnamon, garam masala, ginger and
   mace to a large bowl and season with salt and black pepper. Dredge
   the meat in the flour, reserving any flour that is left.
3 Add 2 tablespoons of oil to a large saucepan and set over a medium-
   high heat. Brown the beef in batches, taking care not to overcrowd
   the pan. Set the cooked meat aside on a large plate and add the next
   batch, adding more oil if needed.

4 Add the onion to the pan and cook for 5 minutes. Add the carrots and the remaining spiced flour and cook for a further 5 minutes.

5 Reduce the heat to medium and pour in the red wine and beef stock. Scrape the bottom of the pan with a spoon to dislodge any flour sticking to the bottom.

6 Add the beef, cover the pan with a lid, then simmer over a low heat for 1 hour, stirring occasionally. If the mixture starts to catch on the bottom of the pan, add a splash of water. (The pie filling should be thick so don't add too much extra liquid.)

7 Meanwhile, make the pastry. Sift the flour into a large bowl, add a good pinch of salt and, using your fingertips, rub in the lard until the mixture resembles fine breadcrumbs. Add the water, a little at a time, and knead lightly to form a ball of dough. Wrap with cling film and chill for at least 30 minutes.

8 Preheat the oven to 200°C/180°C fan/gas mark 6. Wash, quarter, core and thinly slice the apple.

9 Spoon the pie filling into a 1-litre ovenproof dish and stir in the apple.

10 Remove the dough from the fridge. Roll the pastry out on a lightly floured surface until large enough to cover the pie, with room to spare. Cut thin strips of pastry to line the edge of the pie dish and brush with water to moisten. Cover with the pastry lid and press down around the rim of the pie with a fork to seal. Trim off the excess pastry then re-roll your trimmings to make a decoration, if you wish.

11 Add the egg and water to a small bowl and whisk to make an egg wash. Brush heavily over the top of the pie, then use a small, sharp knife to make a couple of small cuts in the centre of the lid to act as vents.

12 Bake for 40–45 minutes, until the pastry is golden brown. Serve with mashed potato.

ꝆEAFY ᵂINTER ЅALAD WITH ᵂALNUTS & ᵇALSAMIC ᴀPPLE ᵛINAIGRETTE

SERVES: 4, AS A SIDE SALAD • PREP TIME: 5 MINUTES •
COOK TIME: 5—6 MINUTES

This simple side salad takes just minutes to put together but is so tasty.

Handful of walnut halves
Drizzle of olive oil, for toasting
120g salad leaves (a mixture of
  watercress, spinach and rocket
  works well)
1 medium crisp dessert apple (try
  Barnack Beauty, Cox's Orange
  Pippin, Sturmer Pippin or
  Tydeman's Late Orange)
100g blue cheese, such as Stilton or
  Roquefort, crumbled (optional)

**BALSAMIC APPLE
VINAIGRETTE**
3 tbsp walnut oil
1 tbsp apple balsamic
  vinegar
Good pinch of freshly
  ground black pepper
Pinch of sea salt

1 Heat the oven to 180°C/160°C fan/gas mark 4. Spread the walnuts
  out on a baking sheet and drizzle with a little olive oil. Bake for
  5–6 minutes, until lightly toasted. Remove from the oven and
  set aside.
2 Add the salad leaves to a large bowl. Then pour all the ingredients
  for the vinaigrette into a small, screwtop jar. Shake to combine and
  then use it to dress the leaves.
3 Wash, quarter, core and thinly slice the apple, peel on, and add to
  the bowl. Scatter over the walnuts and, if using, top with crumbled
  cheese. Serve immediately.

APPLE & CELERIAC RÉMOULADE

SERVES: 4 • PREP TIME: 15 MINUTES, PLUS 30 MINUTES RESTING

A French winter salad combining the subtle, celery-like flavour
of celeriac with sweet-sharp apples in a creamy dressing. Serve it
as a side with Serrano ham and watercress, on toast, or as part of a
lunchtime platter.

1 medium celeriac, about 450g
2 medium sweet dessert apples
   (try crisp Barnack Beauty,
   Kidd's Orange Red, Thoday's
   Quarrenden or William Crump)
Juice of ½ lemon
4 heaped tbsp mayonnaise
2 tbsp Dijon mustard
2 tbsp crème fraîche

2 tbsp parsley, finely chopped
Salt and freshly ground black
   pepper, to taste
Handful of toasted walnuts,
   coarsely chopped

TO SERVE
4–6 slices Serrano ham
Bunch of watercress

1 Peel and slice the celeriac into thin matchsticks. Wash, core and slice
   the apples into thin matchsticks, peel on. Add the celeriac and apple
   to a large bowl along with the lemon juice and toss well to coat. (The
   acidity of the lemon juice tenderises the celeriac and prevents the apple
   and celeriac browning.)
2 Mix the mayonnaise, mustard, crème fraîche and parsley together
   in a small bowl. Season with salt and black pepper and fold into
   the apple and celeriac along with the chopped walnuts. Set aside for
   30 minutes to allow the flavours to meld. Serve with Serrano ham
   and watercress.

APPLE & MARZIPAN TARTLETS

MAKES: 12 MINI TARTS • PREP TIME: 15 MINUTES, PLUS 30 MINUTES CHILLING • COOK TIME: 20 MINUTES

These delightful little tarts combine sweet marzipan with apple in a pastry case. A tasty teatime treat.

PASTRY
250g plain flour, plus extra
    for dusting
Pinch of salt
125g butter, softened, plus
    extra for greasing
1–2 tbsp cold water

FRANGIPANE
50g caster sugar
50g butter

1 egg
50g ground almonds
1 tsp finely grated lemon zest

FILLING
1 medium well-flavoured dessert
    apple (try Calville Blanc d'Hiver,
    Maclean's Favourite, Sanspareil
    or Tydeman's Late Orange)
125g marzipan, cut into 5mm
    (¼-inch) cubes

1 First, make the pastry. Sift the flour into a medium bowl and add a pinch of salt. Using your fingertips, rub in the butter until the mixture resembles fine breadcrumbs. Add the water, a little at a time, and knead lightly to form a ball of dough. Cover with cling film and chill for at least 30 minutes.

2 Next, prepare the frangipane. Cream together the sugar and butter until light and fluffy. Add the egg and mix until well combined then fold in the ground almonds and lemon zest.

3 Peel, core and chop the apple into small pieces (about 5mm/¼-inch cubes is ideal). Add to a small bowl and mix in the marzipan.

4 Preheat the oven to 200°C/180°C fan/gas mark 6. Butter a 12-hole tart tin.

continued

5 Remove the dough from the fridge and roll out onto a lightly floured surface to just under the thickness of a £1 coin. Use a 10cm (4 inch) round cutter to stamp out 12 large circles and a 5cm (2 inch) cutter to stamp out 12 smaller ones, re-rolling the pastry if necessary.

6 Use the larger pastry rounds to line the prepared tart tin. Add a heaped teaspoon of the frangipane to each of the pastry cases and top with the apple and marzipan, pressing down gently to pack as much of the mixture in as possible. Pop the smaller pastry rounds on top.

7 Bake for 15–20 minutes, until the pastry is golden.

8 Cool in the tin for 5 minutes before carefully turning out onto a wire rack to cool completely. *Store in an airtight container for up to 3 days.*

Eve's Pudding

SERVES: 6 • PREP TIME: 25 MINUTES • COOK TIME: 40–45 MINUTES

A comforting, quintessentially British pud of baked apples topped with a light sponge.

3 large Bramley apples
Pinch of grated nutmeg
120g raisins
170g unsalted butter, plus extra
    for greasing

85g light brown soft sugar
3 large eggs
170g self-raising flour

Custard, to serve

1 Preheat the oven to 180°C/160°C fan/gas mark 4. Grease a 1.5–1.75-litre ovenproof dish.

2 Peel, core and finely slice the apples and add to the prepared dish. Sprinkle with the nutmeg and scatter the raisins on top.

3 Cream the butter and sugar together in a bowl until light and fluffy. Stir in the eggs and then carefully fold in the flour with a large metal spoon.

4 Spoon the mixture over the fruit and bake for 40–45 minutes, until golden and springy to the touch, or until a skewer inserted into the sponge comes out clean. Serve warm with custard.

PIPPIN PIE

SERVES: 6–8 • PREP TIME: 20 MINUTES, PLUS 30 MINUTES CHILLING • COOK TIME: 40–50 MINUTES

Pippin Pie dates back to the time of Queen Anne when the 'fairest and best Pippens' were flavoured with sweet spices and encased in suet to make little pies. Traditionally, this recipe was made using the whole apple, peel, pips and all but that's taking it a little far for me.

This version is an adaptation of a recipe recreated for Audley End Apple Festival near Saffron Waldon, in Essex, from the cookbook of Jemima, Marchioness Grey, c.1740–60. The original recipe uses puff pastry and a splash more wine, and though in general more wine is a good thing, I prefer a slightly firmer set filling and classic shortcrust pastry.

PASTRY

500g plain flour, plus extra
   for dusting
Pinch of salt
125g butter, softened, plus extra
   for greasing
125g vegetable fat (such as
   Trex or Cookeen), cut
   into cubes
35g ground almonds
½ tsp almond extract
3–4 tbsp cold water, more
   if needed

1 egg, beaten with 2 tbsp water,
   for glazing

FILLING

6 medium dessert apples,
   preferably pippins (try Cox's
   Orange Pippin, Christmas
   Pippin® or Ribston Pippin)
120g amaretti biscuits
3 tbsp white wine
3 egg yolks
Finely grated zest and juice of
   1 unwaxed lemon
100g butter, cut into cubes

Custard, to serve

EQUIPMENT

Hand blender

continued

1 First, make the pastry. Sift the flour into a large bowl, add a good pinch of salt and, using your fingertips, rub in the butter and vegetable fat until the mixture resembles fine breadcrumbs. Stir in the ground almonds and almond extract. Add the water, a little at a time, and knead lightly to form a ball of dough. Wrap tightly with cling film and chill for at least 30 minutes.

2 Preheat the oven to 200°C/180°C fan/gas mark 6. Grease a 20cm (8 inch) loose-bottomed cake tin and lightly dust with flour.

3 Peel, core and roughly chop the apples. Place in a lightly greased baking dish and bake until tender, 10–15 minutes. Remove from the oven and whizz with a hand blender until smooth.

4 Add the biscuits to a polythene bag and crush with a rolling pin, until broken into small pieces. Stir into the apple along with the white wine, egg yolks, lemon zest and juice and butter. Whisk until thoroughly blended.

5 Remove the dough from the fridge. Roll two-thirds of the pastry out on a lightly floured surface to the thickness of a £1 coin and use it to line the bottom of the tin, leaving any overhang for the time being. Prick the bottom with a fork.

6 Spoon the apple filling into the pie shell.

7 Roll out the remaining pastry until large enough to cover the pie, with room to spare. Using a small, sharp knife, cut the pastry into long strips (10 × 1cm/½-inch-thick strips is ideal).

8 Brush the rim of the pie shell with water and then weave the strips of pastry evenly over the fruit filling to create a lattice pattern. (Or, for a simpler way, lay half the strips at 3cm (1⅛-inch) intervals across the top of the pie, turn the cake tin 90 degrees, and repeat with the remaining strips to create a lattice effect.) Press down all the way round the edge to seal. Trim the overhang of pastry.

9 Add the egg and water to a small bowl and whisk to make an egg wash and heavily brush over the lattice top.

10 Bake for 30–35 minutes, until the pastry is golden. Serve warm with custard.

APPLE & CIDER BREAD PUDDING

SERVES: 6–8 • PREP TIME: 20 MINUTES, PLUS CHILLING OVERNIGHT •
COOK TIME: 35–40 MINUTES

A tempting twist on the classic pud with chunks of apple, cider and
warming spices.

400ml dry English cider
200g golden caster sugar
½ tsp ground cinnamon
½ tsp mixed spice
50g sultanas
50g raisins
Zest of ½ orange
8 slices of day-old bread
50g butter, plus extra for greasing

2 large well-flavoured apples
(I prefer varieties that keep
their shape when cooked such
as Ashmead's Kernel, Howgate
Wonder or Sanspareil)
3 eggs, beaten
1 tbsp Demerara sugar

Custard or cream, to serve

1 Add the cider, caster sugar, spices, dried fruits and orange zest to
   a small saucepan. Bring to the boil and simmer for 2–3 minutes.
   Remove from the heat, pour into a large bowl and set aside to cool.
2 Tear the bread into small pieces and stir into the cider mixture.
   Cover the bowl with cling film and refrigerate overnight.
3 Preheat the oven to 180°C/160°C fan/gas mark 4 and grease a
   1.5–1.75-litre ovenproof dish. Peel, quarter, core and coarsely chop
   the apples (I prefer to keep the pieces quite large).
4 Add the butter to a frying pan and melt over a medium heat. Fry the
   apples until lightly coloured, 3–4 minutes. Then set aside to cool.
5 Remove the bread mixture from the fridge and stir in the eggs. Fold in
   the apple and spoon the mixture into the prepared dish. Sprinkle the
   Demerara sugar over the top.
6 Bake for 35–40 minutes, until golden brown. Serve warm with custard
   or cream.

APPLE STRUDEL

SERVES: 8 • PREP TIME: 35 MINUTES, PLUS 30 MINUTES SOAKING •
COOK TIME: 35–40 MINUTES

This richly-flavoured, boozy version of the Austrian classic is perfect for winter – served, of course, with *kaffee*.

There is some debate about which type of apple works best in a strudel. A lot of recipes recommend using culinary varieties that cook to a purée but I prefer my fruit to retain a little bite. Here, I like to use a combination of sweet-sharp Howgate Wonder and dry, nutty russets.

PASTRY

Four 25 × 45cm (10 × 17¾ inches) sheets of filo pastry
60g butter, melted
15g flaked almonds
Icing sugar, for dusting

FILLING

125g sultanas
50ml cider brandy or Calvados (optional)
400g cooking apple (try Annie Elizabeth or Howgate Wonder)

400g russet apple (try Brownlees Russet, Rosemary Russet or Egremont Russet)
Finely grated zest and juice of 1 large unwaxed lemon
3 tbsp light muscovado sugar
½ tsp ground cinnamon
½ tsp mixed spice
Pinch of salt
60g blanched almonds, finely chopped (aim for a fine 'gravel')

Whipped cream or vanilla ice cream, to serve

1 If using cider brandy or Calvados, add the sultanas to a medium bowl and pour over the cider brandy. Stir to coat the fruit and leave to soak for 20–30 minutes.

2 Preheat the oven to 190°C/170°C fan/gas mark 5. Grease a large baking sheet.

3 While the sultanas are soaking, peel, core and slice the apples. Aim for fairly uniform pieces, around 5mm (¼-inch) thick. (If using Egremont Russets you may find it easier to remove the core using a knife rather than using an apple corer as the flesh can be quite brittle.)

4 Add the apple and lemon zest and juice to a large bowl and sift in the muscovado sugar, cinnamon and mixed spice. Add a pinch of salt and stir. Next, mix in the chopped, blanched almonds.

5 Drain the excess brandy from the sultanas and add to the bowl. Stir to combine.

6 Next, place 1 sheet of filo pastry on the prepared baking sheet and brush lightly with melted butter. Cover with the remaining sheets, brushing each with butter.

7 Stir the filling again and spoon into a thick strip along the middle third of the pastry.

8 Fold the ends of the pastry in and then tightly wrap over the sides so that the filling is completely enclosed. Gently turn the strudel over on the baking sheet so that the seal is on the bottom. For a traditional touch, bend the ends of the pastry inwards to make a horseshoe shape.

9 Brush the top of the strudel with melted butter and sprinkle with flaked almonds. Bake for 35–40 minutes, until the pastry is crisp and golden. Remove from the oven and dust with icing sugar. Serve just warm with whipped cream or vanilla ice cream. *Store in the fridge for up to 4 days, loosely covered with foil or cling film.*

VARIATION

For a delicious alternative, why not try pear and date strudel? Simply substitute the apples with the equivalent weight in pears (800g is equivalent to about 6 large Comice pears), peeled, cored and thickly sliced; replace the cider-brandy infused sultanas with 125g Medjool dates, pitted and roughly chopped; and use ground ginger in place of the cinnamon. Again, try to keep the fruit slices a fairly uniform size so that they cook at the same rate (roughly 5mm/¼-inch thick is ideal).

Sticky Apple & Ginger Upside-Down Pudding

SERVES: 6 • PREP TIME: 15 MINUTES • COOK TIME: 30–35 MINUTES

A modern take on the retro favourite, pineapple upside-down cake. This dessert is deliciously sweet and gooey like sticky toffee.

TOPPING

3 medium apples (try Annie Elizabeth, aromatic D'Arcy Spice or Lord Hindlip)

50g butter, softened, plus more for frying

50g light brown soft sugar

CAKE

100g butter, softened and cut into cubes

100g caster sugar (I like golden caster sugar but white caster sugar is fine)

1 tsp vanilla extract (optional)

2 eggs

4 tbsp golden syrup

125g self-raising flour

1 tsp baking powder

½ tsp ground cinnamon

¼ tsp mixed spice

¼ tsp grated nutmeg

Pinch of salt

2 tbsp stem ginger in syrup, finely grated

Cream or vanilla ice cream, to serve

1 Preheat oven to 180°C/160°C fan/gas mark 4 and grease a 20cm (8 inch) round cake tin.
2 First make the topping: wash and core the apples, peel on. Slice two and a half apples into 1cm (½-inch) thick rounds, reserving the remaining half an apple for the cake batter.
3 Heat a little butter in a frying pan and add half of the sliced apple. Cook over a medium heat, turning the apples over once or twice until the slices are just tender, about 2 minutes. Remove the cooked apple and repeat with the remaining slices. Set aside to cool.

continued

4 Using the same pan, heat the 50g butter and soft brown sugar together, stirring constantly until the butter has melted and the sugar has dissolved. Cook over a high heat, swirling often, until large bubbles that are slow to pop form. Pour the mixture into the cake tin and tilt the tin to coat the bottom evenly.

5 Arrange the cooked apple slices in overlapping layers on top and set aside.

6 To make the cake: cream the butter and sugar together in a medium bowl until light and fluffy. Add the vanilla extract, if using, and eggs, then stir in the golden syrup. Mix the dry ingredients (flour, baking powder, spices and salt) together in a separate bowl and then gradually add the dry mix to the wet. Stir until fully combined and lump-free. Finely chop the reserved half an apple and gently fold into the mix along with the grated stem ginger.

7 Spoon the cake batter into the tin on top of the apple and level out the top. Bake for 30–35 minutes, until brown and a skewer inserted into the cake comes out almost clean.

8 Remove from the oven and leave to cool in the tin for 5 minutes. Run the blade of a sharp knife all the way around the edge of the tin to loosen the pudding. Place a large plate over the tin and gently invert the tin on to the plate and lift the tin off. Serve warm with cream or vanilla ice cream. *Store at room temperature for up to 24 hours, with the top tightly wrapped with cling film.*

ᴀPPLE ꜱTOLLEN

SERVES: 6–8 • PREP TIME: 30 MINUTES,
PLUS 2 HOURS 30 MINUTES PROVING • COOK TIME: 1 HOUR

It is said that the shape of the stollen was meant to represent the Christ
Child wrapped in swaddling clothes, which is why it is traditionally
made at Christmas. This is my tasty twist on the favourite festive fruit
bread. It's simple to make, although it does take a little time.

250g strong white bread flour,
   plus extra for dusting
40g caster sugar
I tsp fast-action yeast
½ tsp salt
75g unsalted butter, softened
125ml whole milk
75g dried fruit, such as raisins
   and currants
2 tbsp blanched almonds, chopped
Few drops of vanilla extract
2 drops of almond extract
Pinch of grated nutmeg

20ml cider brandy or Calvados
   (optional)
2 tbsp butter, melted, for brushing
110g marzipan
I tsp icing sugar, for dusting

FILLING

I dessert apple (try aromatic
   Ashmead's Kernel, Cornish
   Gilliflower, D'Arcy Spice or
   William Crump)
I tbsp caster sugar
½ tsp ground cinnamon

1 Sift the flour and sugar into a large bowl and add the yeast and salt.
   Add the butter and most of the milk and stir to combine.
2 Add the remaining milk and mix to form a soft dough.
3 Turn out on to a well-floured surface and knead for 6–7 minutes,
   until smooth.
4 Add the dried fruit, almonds, vanilla and almond extracts, nutmeg
   and cider brandy, if using, to a large bowl. Stir to combine. Drop the
   dough on top and knead from the outside into the centre to incorporate
   the ingredients.

continued

5 Cover with cling film and place in a warm, draught-free area until the dough has doubled in size, about 1½ hours.

6 Punch the dough down and roll out on a lightly floured surface to a rectangle roughly the same size as your baking sheet. (You may find it easier to roll the dough out on a large sheet of floured baking parchment and use that to transfer the finished stollen to the baking sheet.) Brush with melted butter.

7 Knead the marzipan until pliable then roll out on a lightly floured surface to the same size as the dough. Lay the marzipan on top of the dough.

8 Wash, quarter, core and thinly slice the apple, peel on, and scatter over the marzipan. Sprinkle with the sugar and cinnamon.

9 Roll the dough up into a large sausage shape, enclosing the apple. Lightly press down with the palms of your hands to flatten slightly. Gently turn the stollen over so that the seal is on the bottom, loosely cover with cling film, and leave to rise for 1 hour.

10 Preheat the oven to 190°C/170°C fan/gas mark 5. Line a large baking sheet with baking parchment.

11 When the stollen has risen, transfer to the prepared baking sheet and score the top lightly with a small, sharp knife.

12 Bake on the middle shelf of the oven for an hour, until pale gold and firm to the touch.

13 Remove from the oven, brush well with melted butter and when this has set, dust generously with icing sugar. Leave to cool on the baking sheet for 10 minutes before transferring to a wire rack to cool completely. Serve cold. *Store, wrapped loosely in cling film, in an airtight container for up to 5 days.*

ℋomemade Applesauce

SERVES: 6-8 • PREP TIME: 10 MINUTES • COOK TIME: 15 MINUTES

Homemade applesauce couldn't be simpler and it is so versatile.
It can be used in cakes and muffins, spread on toast or swirled into
your morning bowl of porridge or served as an accompaniment to
savoury meat or cheese dishes.

3-4 large Bramley apples, about   50g caster sugar
    750g (or try Bramley 20,   50g butter
    Edward VII or Emneth Early)

1 Peel, quarter, core and roughly chop the apples. Add to a medium
saucepan along with the sugar and butter and cover with a lid. Cook
over a low heat, stirring occasionally, until the apples have broken
down into a purée, about 15 minutes. Mash with a fork to remove any
remaining lumps and spoon into a serving dish. *Store covered in the
fridge for up to a week.*

VARIATIONS

To serve with chicken: add a pinch of ground ginger or nutmeg and
the juice of 1 small lemon.

To serve with pork or ham: add 1 tablespoon of honey.

To serve with duck: add 1 teaspoon of ground cinnamon and warm
through with a star anise and a couple of cloves, or try adding 100g of
fresh blackberries to the basic recipe.

To serve with goose: try adding the juice of 1 small lemon and a couple
of cloves.

BLACKBERRY & APPLE CRUMBLE SMOOTHIE

SERVES: 2–3 • PREP TIME: 10 MINUTES

A delicious, fruity, fibre-rich way to start the day. Dessert for breakfast, where do I sign?

1 medium apple (try Ashmead's Kernel, Brownlees' Russet or D'Arcy Spice)

300g frozen mixed berries (using frozen berries is cheaper than using fresh fruits and helps to thicken the smoothie)

200ml semi-skimmed milk

150g fat-free natural yoghurt

2 tbsp porridge oats

1 tbsp flaked almonds

¼ tsp ground cinnamon

Pinch of grated nutmeg

75ml still mineral water

1 Peel, core and coarsely chop the apple. Then add all the ingredients, except the mineral water, to the bowl of a food processor and blend until smooth. Add the mineral water, a little at a time, and blend again. Pour into glasses and enjoy.

TIP

For a dairy-free version, substitute the milk and yoghurt for 2 small ripe bananas and add extra mineral water to your desired consistency.

Apple, Pear & Ginger Smoothie

SERVES: 2 • PREP TIME: 10 MINUTES

Show winter sniffles the door with this sweet, nutrient-rich smoothie.

I medium apple (try Cox's Orange
  Pippin, Gala or Jonagold)
I ripe pear
I tsp lemon juice

I tsp finely grated fresh ginger
250g fat-free natural yoghurt
I tbsp clear runny honey,
  plus extra to taste

1 Peel, core and coarsely chop the apple and pear. Then add all the ingredients to the bowl of a food processor and blend until smooth. Check for sweetness and add a little extra honey, if you like. Pour into glasses and serve.

TIP

Try adding a few spinach leaves to the mix. The spinach adds a lovely touch of extra colour to the juice and added nutrients without changing the flavour.

𝒜 TO 𝒵 OF 𝒱ARIETIES

The total number of cultivated apple varieties is said to be around 7,500 worldwide, although no-one really knows for certain. This figure appears regularly on websites and in various books and, as such, has become something of a received wisdom. However, whatever the actual figure it would be impractical to include them all here. Even the UK figure alone – over 2,200 in number – would be too lengthy a list for a book of this sort. Therefore I have hand-picked around 250 varieties that I believe best represent the rich apple-producing heritage still grown in the UK and Ireland, as well as a few of the usual suspects found on supermarket shelves.

(c) = culinary apple
(d) = dessert apple
(s) = cider apple
(h) = good keeping variety

Acklam Russet *(d)* Mid October. Originated from Acklam, Yorkshire and recorded in 1768. Fruits have firm flesh with a sweet to moderately sharp flavour.

Acme *(d)* Mid September. Raised in 1944 at Boreham, Essex by W. Seabrook & Sons Ltd. Fruits have firm flesh with a slightly perfumed flavour. Parentage: Worcester Pearmain X Rival x Cox's Orange Pippin.

Adams's Pearmain *(d/h)* Early October. Introduced and exhibited by R. Adams of Herefordshire in 1826. A popular Edwardian and Victorian dessert apple. Fruits are juicy, slightly sweet with a pleasant aromatic flavour. Synonyms: Hanging Pearmain, Lady's Finger, Matchless, Moriker, Norfolk Pippin, Norfolk Russet, Rough Pippin, Winter Striper Pearmain.

Admiral *(d)* Early October. Raised in about 1921 at Upton, Norfolk by A. K. Watson from seed brought back from Japan. It was introduced in around 1937. Fruits have coarse flesh with a sweet flavour.

Aldenham Blenheim *(c/d)* Late September. It was discovered before 1929 at Aldenham House, Hertfordshire by Head Gardener, Edwin Beckett and is believed to be a coloured sport of Blenheim Orange. Fruits have rather dry flesh with a rich aromatic flavour.

Alfriston *(c/k)* Early October. Raised in the late 1700s by Mr Shepherd at Uckfield, Sussex and named 'Shepherd's Pippin'. It was renamed Alfriston in 1819 after a Mr Booker of Alfriston, Sussex, sent it to the London Horticultural Society. Fruits have coarse-textured, acidic flesh which cooks to a purée. Offspring: Morley's Seedling. Synonyms: Green Goose, Lord Gwydyr's Newton Pippin, Shepherd's Seedling.

Alkmene *(d)* Late September. Raised in 1930 at Brandenburg, Germany and named 'Alkamenein'. Introduced to the UK in 1962 and renamed Early Windsor for the UK market in 1996. Fruits are crisp and juicy with a Cox-like flavour. Sports: Red Alkmene (renamed Red Windsor in 1998).

Allington Pippin *(d/k)* Early October. Raised by solicitor Thomas Laxton in Lincolnshire before 1884. It received a First Class Certificate from the Royal Horticultural Society in 1894 under its original name, 'Brown's South Lincoln Beauty'. It was renamed in 1894 by nurseryman George Bunyard after the village of Allington, near Maidstone, Kent, where one of his nurseries was situated and introduced by him in 1896. Fruits have an aromatic flavour. Parentage: King of the Pippins x Cox's Orange Pippin. Offspring: Cheddar Cross, John Huggett, Plymouth Cross.

Annie Elizabeth *(c/k)* Early October. Raised by Samuel Greatorex at Knighton, Leicester in about 1857 and named after his baby daughter. Introduced in about 1898. A good, late-keeping culinary apple which keeps its shape when cooked. Synonyms: Carter's Seedling, Sussex Pippin, The George.

Api *(d)* Mid October. Also known as 'Lady Apple'. It is thought to have been found in the Forest of Apis in Brittany, France. Recorded in 1628. Fruits are sweet, crisp and juicy with an aromatic flavour. Synonyms: Apis, Appease, Christmas Apple, Lady.

Arthur Turner *(c)* Late September. Raised by Charles Turner at Slough, at that time part of Buckinghamshire, and introduced by him in 1915. Received the Award of Merit from the Royal Horticultural Society in 1912 as 'Turner's Prolific'. It was renamed in 1913. A large culinary apple noted for its particularly attractive blossom. Fruits cook to a sweet purée.

Arthur W. Barnes *(c)* Mid September. Raised in 1902 by N. F. Barnes, Head Gardener to the Duke of Westminster at Eaton Gardens, Chester. Introduced in 1928 by Clibrans of Altrincham. Fruits cook to a well-flavoured purée. Parentage: Gascoyne's Scarlet x Cox's Orange Pippin.

Ashmead's Kernel *(d/k)* Early October. Generally said to have been raised in about 1700 by Dr Ashmead of Gloucester, although some sources give his name and occupation as Mr Ashmead, attorney at law and later town clerk. Fruits have firm, juicy flesh with a rich aromatic flavour. Synonyms: Ashmead's Samling, Ashmead's Seedling.

Autumn Harvest *(c/d)* Late August. Thought to have originated from Westmorland in north-west England. Recorded in 1934. Fruits have firm, dry flesh with a subacid flavour.

Autumn Pearmain *(d)* Late September. An English dessert variety known to have been in existence in the late 1500s. Fruits have a pleasant, slightly aromatic flavour. Synonyms: Arthur Sheen, Drue Pearmain, Summer Pearmain, Summer Pippin.

Baker's Delicious *(d)* Early September. Found in South Wales and introduced by Baker's of Codsall, Wolverhampton, in 1932. Fruits are crisp and juicy with an aromatic flavour.

Ball's Pippin *(d)* Early October. Introduced in 1923 by J. C. Allgrove, Langley, then part of Buckinghamshire. Fruits are sweet and crisp. Parentage: Cox's Orange Pippin x Sturmer Pippin. Synonyms: Lane's Oakland Seedling.

Ballyfatten *(c)* Late September. Originated from Northern Ireland and first recorded in 1802. Fruits have firm flesh with an acid flavour.

Barnack Beauty *(d/k)* Early October. Raised at Barnack, Cambridgeshire in about 1840 and introduced around 1870 by nurserymen W. and J. Brown of nearby Stamford. Fruits are sweet, crisp and juicy with a good flavour. A long-keeping variety. Offspring: Barnack Orange, Jennifer Wastie.

Barnack Orange *(d)* Early October. Raised in 1904 at Belvoir Castle, Leicestershire, by W. H. Divers. Fruits have firm, coarse-textured flesh and a good aromatic flavour. Parentage: Barnack Beauty x Cox's Orange Pippin.

Beauty of Bath *(d)* Early August. Raised at Bailbrook, Bath, Somerset and introduced by George Cooling of Bath in about 1864. It was once an important early commercial apple in the UK. Fruits are juicy, sweet and a little acidic with a distinctive flavour. Sports: Crimson Beauty of Bath.

Beauty of Hants *(d)* Early October. Raised by Mrs Eyre Crabbe at Bassett, Southampton, Hampshire prior to 1850. It is said to be a seedling from Blenheim Orange open-pollinated. Fruits have a pleasant flavour similar to Blenheim Orange.

Beauty of Kent *(c)* Late September. Thought to be of English origin and introduced in about 1820. Fruits are juicy and subacid with a faint pleasant flavour. Synonyms: Gadd's Seedling, Kentish Broading, Kentish Pippin, Wooling's Favourite.

Beauty of Stoke *(c)* Mid October. Raised by Mr Doe, Head Gardener to Lord Saville at Rufford Abbey, Nottinghamshire and introduced by Veitch & Sons Nurseries. Recorded in 1889. Fruits have coarse, dry flesh with a subacid flavour.

Bedwyn Beauty *(c)* Mid October. Raised by farmer Mr Stone of Great Bedwyn, near Marlborough, Wiltshire around 1890. Fruits have firm, coarse flesh with a sweetish flavour.

Belle de Boskoop *(c/d)* Early October. Found by K. J. W. Ottolander in Boskoop, South Holland in 1856. Fruits have firm flesh with a pleasant, aromatic flavour.

Belvoir Seedling *(d)* Early October. Raised by W. H. Divers, probably at Belvoir Castle, Leicestershire. Fruits have firm flesh with a sweet to subacid flavour. Parentage: Annie Elizabeth x Dumelow's Seedling.

Ben's Red *(d)* Early September. Raised by Benjamin Roberts at Trannack, Cornwall in about 1830. Fruits have firm flesh with a sweet, pleasant flavour. Parentage: Devonshire Quarrenden x Farleigh Pippin.

Benenden Early *(d)* Mid August. Raised in around 1945 at Southampton, Hampshire by J. J. Gibbons and introduced in 1952 by Stuart Low Ltd. of Benenden, Kent. Fruits have soft flesh with a subacid flavour. Parentage: Saint Edmund's Pippin x Lady Sudeley.

Bess Pool *(d/k)* Early October. Discovered in a wood in Nottinghamshire by Bess Pool. It was first recorded in 1824 and introduced by nurseryman J. R. Pearson of Chilwell, Nottinghamshire. Fruits have somewhat dry flesh with a sweet and pleasant flavour. Synonyms: Old Bess Pool, Ronald's Besspool, Stradbroke Pippin, Walsgrove Blenheim. Offspring: New Bess Pool.

Blenheim Orange *(c/d)* Late September. A popular old English variety discovered by tailor George Kempster in Woodstock near Blenheim, Oxfordshire, in about 1740. Distributed in about 1818. It is known locally as 'Dempster's Pippin' [sic]. Fruits have somewhat coarse, dry flesh with a rich aromatic flavour. Synonyms: Beauty of Dumbleton, Bleinheim Pippin, Woodstock Pippin. Offspring: Annie Elizabeth, Beauty of Hants, Edward VII, Howgate Wonder, Newton Wonder.

Bloody Ploughman *(d)* Mid September. Originated from Carse of Gowrie, Scotland. Recorded in 1883. It has been claimed that its name comes from a ploughman who was caught scrumping apples in the grounds of Megginch Castle and was shot by the gamekeeper but is more likely to be for the blood red colour of its skin when fully ripe. Fruits have crisp flesh with a slightly sweet, subacid flavour.

Blue Pearmain *(d)* Early October. Thought to have originated from USA. It was known in the early 1800s. Its name comes from a dusty bluish coating or 'bloom' covering the skin. Fruits have somewhat dry, soft flesh with a sweet, pleasant aromatic flavour.

Bountiful *(c/d/k)* Late September. Introduced by East Malling Research Station, Kent, in 1964. It is relatively sweet and has an excellent flavour when cooked.

Braddick's Nonpareil *(d)* Mid October. Raised by John Braddick at Thames Ditton, Surrey. First exhibited in 1818. Fruits have firm flesh with a sweet, aromatic flavour. Synonyms: Ditton Nonpareil, Ditton Pippin.

Braeburn *(d)* Late October. Discovered on the property of O. Moran, Upper Moutere, New Zealand and first grown commercially by William Bros. at Braeburn Orchards, Upper Moutere in 1952. Fruits have crisp, firm flesh with a perfumed flavour, although fruits usually fail to mature fully in the UK. This variety stores very well. Parentage: Lady Hamilton x Unknown. Offspring: JAZZ™, Kanzi®.

Bramley's Seedling (Bramley) *(c/k)* Early October. Raised by a young Mary Ann Brailsford in the garden of her home in Southwell, Nottinghamshire between 1809 and 1813. The property was sold to butcher Matthew Bramley in 1846, and, a decade later, when nurseryman H. Merryweather approached Bramley to ask if he could take cuttings and begin to sell the apples, Bramley agreed with the stipulation that the apple be named after him. It was introduced by Merryweather in 1865. Bramley's Seedling is currently the most popular cooking apple grown in the UK, representing more than 95% of all apples sold for cooking in the home. Fruits have acid flesh which cooks to a smooth purée. Synonyms: Bramley, Bramleys Samling. Offspring: Woolbrook Russet. Sports: Bramley 20.

Breadfruit *(c/d)* Early October. Originated from Rezare, Cornwall in about 1900. The name comes from the fruit's white flesh. Fruits have a sweet, aromatic flavour with a hint of strawberry when ripe.

Brithmawr Forester *(c/d/s)* Mid September. Originated from South Wales. Fruits have an acid flavour.

Broad-eyed Pippin (of Bultitude) *(c)* Early September. Raised in England and recorded in the late 1600s. Fruits have moderately firm, coarse-textured flesh and are juicy and acid.

Broadholme Beauty *(c/d)* Late September. Raised in Broadholme, Lincolnshire in about 1995 by Henry Lovely. Fruits are juicy with a mild, sweet flavour. Keeps its shape when cooked. This variety is noted for being particularly high in natural sugar, making them a good choice for diabetics as little or no sugar is needed for cooking. Parentage: James Grieve x Lane's Prince Albert.

Brown's Seedling (c/d/k) Mid October. Raised before 1874 by nurserymen W. and J. Brown at Stamford, Lincolnshire. Fruits have a sweet to moderately sharp flavour. Cooks to a textured purée.

Brownlees' Russet (d/k) Mid October. Raised in England and introduced by William Brownlees of Hemel Hempstead, Hertfordshire in about 1848. Fruits are juicy and somewhat acid, with a pleasant nutty flavour.

Bulmer's Norman (s) Mid October. Originally an unnamed variety imported from Normandy, France. It was developed by H. P. Bulmer & Co., Ltd., in Hereford. Fruits produce a bittersweet, medium cider.

Calville Blanc d'Hiver (c/d) Mid October. Raised in Europe, probably France or Germany and recorded in 1598. Fruits have juicy flesh with a rich, sweet, aromatic flavour. Fruits fail to ripen fully in the UK. Calville Blanc d'Hiver is considered to be one of the top culinary varieties. Synonyms: Paris Apple, White Autumn Calville, White Calville, Winter Calville.

Cameo® (d) Early October. A modern commercial variety discovered as a chance seedling by the Caudle family in Dryden, Washington, USA in 1987. Fruits have soft flesh with a sweet flavour. Its parentage is uncertain but it is thought to be Red Delicious x Golden Delicious. Synonyms: Caudle.

Captain Kidd (d) Mid October. A more highly coloured sport of Kidd's Orange Red. Originated in 1962 in the orchard of Robin Osborne at Twyford, Hawkes Bay, New Zealand. Introduced in 1969. Fruits are crisp, sweet and juicy with a rich, aromatic flavour.

Catshead (c) Early October. Originated from England and known in the 1600s. Fruits have a distinctly angular shape with dry flesh and a moderately sharp flavour. Cooks to a firm purée. Synonyms: Cat-head Greening, Cat's Head Apple, Catshead Round, Green Costard, Herefordshire Goose, Loggerhead, Monstrous, Royal Costard, Tankard, Terwin's Goliath, Tête du Chat (of Jersey). Offspring: Peasgood's Nonsuch, Lord Derby.

Cellini (c/d) Mid September. Raised by Leonard Phillips, a nurseryman at Vauxhall, London and introduced in about 1828. Fruits have rather soft, juicy flesh with a slightly acid flavour. Parentage: Nonsuch x Unknown. Synonyms: Centennial, Norfolk Challenger, Phillips' Seedling.

Charles Ross (c/d) Mid September. Raised by Charles Ross at Welford Park Gardens, near Newbury, Berkshire. It was first exhibited in 1890 as 'Thomas Andrew Knight' but renamed Charles Ross at the request of his employer, Captain Carstairs, in 1899. Fruits are rather coarse-textured, juicy and sweet with a moderate flavour. Keeps its shape when cooked. Parentage: Peasgood's Nonsuch x Cox's Orange Pippin. Sports: Red Charles Ross.

Cheddar Cross *(d)* Late August. Raised in 1916 by G. T. Spinks at Long Ashton Research Station, Bristol and introduced in 1949. Fruits have firm, somewhat acid flesh with little flavour. Parentage: Allington Pippin x Star of Devon.

Chisel Jersey *(s)* Mid November. An old cider variety known to have been widely grown around Martock in Somerset. 'Chisel' is thought to have derived from the old dialect word *chesil*, meaning pebble, in reference to the apple's small size and hardness. 'Jersey' is a term given to bittersweet cider apples in Somerset (the equivalent of 'French' and 'Norman' in Gloucestershire and Herefordshire respectively). According to research on genotyping the apple, the Chisel Jersey is currently believed to be one of the most genetically diverse varieties of *Malus domestica* compared to other cultivars.

Chivers Delight *(d)* Mid October. Raised by John Chivers Farms Ltd., at Histon, Cambridgeshire in around 1926 and introduced in 1936. Fruits are crisp and juicy with a pleasant aromatic flavour.

Christmas Pearmain *(d)* Early October. Raised by Mr Manser and first recorded in 1893. It was introduced by George Bunyard & Co., Maidstone, Kent. Fruits are crisp and juicy with a pleasant aromatic flavour.

Christmas Pippin® *(d)* Early September. A modern commercial variety discovered as a seedling beside the M5 motorway in Somerset in 2003 by Geoffrey Rowson. Introduced in 2010. Its parentage is unknown, although as orchards had once stood in the area it is more likely to have grown from a windfall apple in the original orchard than, as previously thought, as the result of a core tossed from of a passing vehicle. Fruits are crisp and juicy with a sweet, Cox-like flavour.

Civni *see* Rubens®

Clark's Seedling *(c)* Early October. Thought to have originated from the UK. Recorded in 1936. Fruits have soft, coarse flesh with a moderately sharp flavour. Synonyms: Clarke's Pippin, Royal George.

Claygate Pearmain *(d/k)* Early October. Discovered by John Braddick at Claygate, Surrey and exhibited in 1821. Fruits have firm, rather coarse textured juicy flesh with a rich aromatic flavour. Synonyms: Archerfield Pearmain, Bradley's Pearmain, Brown's Pippin, Doncaster Pearmain, Fowler's Pippin, Mason's Ribston Pearmain.

Cockle Pippin *(d)* Mid October. Raised in about 1800 by Mr Cockle at Godstone, Surrey. Fruits have firm somewhat dry flesh with a sweet, pleasant flavour. Synonyms: Brown Cockle, Nutmeg Cockle, White Cockle Pippin.

Coeur de Boeuf *(c)* Mid October. A variety of French origin but known in the UK since 1200s. Fruits have soft flesh with a sweet, subacid, aromatic flavour.

Colonel Vaughan *(d)* Early October. Originated from Kent. It was known in the late 1600s. Fruits have firm flesh with a sweet to subacid flavour. Synonyms: Kentish Pippin, Red Coachman, Scarlet Incomparable.

Colwall Quoining *(d)* Late September. Named after a village in Herefordshire, on the western side of the Malvern Hills. 'Quoining' refers to the corners, the distinct angular ridges of this and other 'quoining' varieties. Fruits have crisp, coarse flesh with a sweet, subacid, nutty flavour.

Cornish Aromatic *(d)* Mid October. Originally found growing in Cornwall. It was brought to notice in 1813 but is thought to be many centuries old. Fruits have firm, rather dry flesh with a rich, aromatic flavour.

Cornish Gilliflower *(d)* Mid October. Found in a cottage garden near Truro, Cornwall. It was introduced by Sir Christopher Hawkins in 1813. Fruits have firm, rather dry flesh with a sweet and rich aromatic flavour. 'Gilliflower' is possibly a corruption of the French word *girofle* meaning clove, thought to be a reference to the fruit's odour when cut. Synonyms: Cornish July Flower, July Flower.

Cottenham Seedling *(c/k)* Mid October. Raised by Robert Norman at Cottenham, Cambridgeshire and introduced by H. J. Gautrey. Fruits have firm, juicy flesh distinctly acid flesh which cooks to a purée. A long-keeping variety. Parentage: Dumelow's Seedling x Unknown.

Court of Wick *(d)* Late September. Originated from Court of Wick, Yatton, Somerset and introduced in 1790 by Wood of Huntingdon. Fruits are crisp with a rich and moderately sharp flavour. Parentage: Golden Pippin x Unknown. Synonyms: Aniseed, Barlow, Kingswick Pippin, Knightwick Pippin, Wick's Pippin, Wood's Transparent, Yellow Pippin.

Court Pendu Plat *(d/k)* Mid October. This variety originated from Europe. It was first described in about 1613 but is believed to be much older. It was also called 'Wise Apple' because it flowers late and escapes spring frost damage. Fruits have an unusual flat shape, firm, juicy flesh with a pleasant, slightly aromatic flavour. Offspring: Oxford Conquest. Synonyms: Coriander Rose, Garnon's Pippin, Russian Apple, Wollaton Pippin.

Cox's Orange Pippin *(d/k)* Late September. Raised in about 1825 by retired brewer Richard Cox at The Lawns (later Colnbrook Lawn), Slough, then part of Buckinghamshire. It was first sold by a Colnbrook nursery, probably E. Small & Son, and introduced by Charles Turner of the Royal Nurseries, Slough, in about 1850. Fruits are juicy and sweet with a rich, aromatic, nutty flavour. Cox's Orange Pippin is regarded as one of the finest dessert apples. Parentage: Ribston Pippin x Unknown. Mother to: Ballard Beauty, Ball's Pippin, Edith Hopwood, Ellison's Orange, Feltham Beauty, Fortune, Jupiter, Kidd's Orange Red, King George V, Merton Pippin, Merton Worcester, Rosy Blenheim, Sunset, Woolbrook Pippin, William Crump. Father to: Acme, Allington Pippin, Arthur W. Barnes, Barnack Orange, Charles Ross, Laxton's Superb, Meridian, Merton Beauty, Merton Prolific, Merton Russet, Rubens, Tydeman's Late Orange. Sports: Crimson Cox, King Cox, Queen Cox, Red Cox.

Cox's Pomona *(c/d)* Mid September. Believed to be a sister seedling of Cox's Orange Pippin. It was raised in about 1825 by retired Bermondsey brewer Richard Cox at The Lawns (later Colnbrook Lawn), Slough, then part of Buckinghamshire, and introduced by E. Small & Son, Slough. Fruits have juicy flesh with a sweet, subacid, fine flavour.

Crab *(c)* Early September. 'Crab apple' is the term used to describe any very small, sour apple. Cultivated varieties do exist but they are more commonly found in the wild. Fruits have very astringent, pectin-rich flesh.

Crawley Beauty *(c/d)* Mid October. Found in a cottage garden in Crawley, Sussex in about 1870 and introduced in 1906 by J. Cheal & Sons, Crawley. It appears to be identical with French variety Nouvelle France. Fruits have rather dry flesh with a subacid, slightly sweet flavour. Cooks to a delicately flavoured purée.

Crawley Reinette *(d)* Mid October. Introduced by J. Cheal & Sons, Crawley, Sussex and recorded in 1902. Fruits have soft flesh with an acid to subacid flavour.

Cripps Pink *(d/k)* Early November. Raised by John Cripps at the (then named) Western Australia Department of Agriculture in 1973 and one of several cultivars from which fruits that meet quality standards can be sold under the trade mark name Pink Lady®. Fruits fail to ripen fully in the UK. Fruits have crisp, juicy flesh with a sweet subacid flavour. Parentage: Lady Williams x Golden Delicious. Sports: Rosy Glow, Lady in Red.

Crispin *see* Mutsu

D'Arcy Spice *(d/k)* Late October. Found at Tolleshunt D'Arcy Hall, Essex, in about 1785, but may be older. It was introduced by John Harris, a nurseryman of Broomfield, Essex, as 'Baddow Pippin' in 1848. Fruits have firm, juicy flesh with a characteristic aromatic flavour. Synonyms: Baddow Pippin, Essex Spice, Spring Ribston Pippin, Winter Ribston.

Dabinett *(s)* Mid November. Thought to have originated from the Martock area of Somerset in the mid-19th century and named after a Mr Dabinett. It is possibly a seedling of Chisel Jersey. Fruits have a sweet, astringent, strong fruity flavour when ripe. A bittersweet variety that produces a full-bodied, high quality cider.

Delbarestivale *see* Delcorf.

Delcorf *(d)* Early September. Raised in the 1956 by nurseryman George Delbard at Malicorne, Allier, France and received by the National Fruit Trials in 1973. It was given the brand name Delbarestival in 1998. Fruits are fairly crisp, juicy and very sweet. Parentage: Golden Delicious x Stark Jonagrimes. Synonyms: Delbard d'Estivale, Delbarestivale, Estivale. Offspring: Zari®.

Delicious *(d)* Early October. An American apple discovered in about 1880 growing from a rootstock by J. Hiatt, near Peru, Iowa. It was introduced by Stark Brothers in 1895. Fruits have very firm, very sweet, juicy flesh with a highly aromatic flavour. Fruits have much better flavour when grown in climates with good temperature and light conditions. Synonyms: Hawkeye, Red Delicious. Offspring: Cameo®, Empire, Fuji, Kidd's Orange Red, Jonalicious. Sport: Richared Delicious™.

Devonshire Quarrenden *(d)* Mid August. Thought to have arisen in Devon, but may in fact have originated from France. It was first recorded in 1678. Fruits are sweet, crisp and juicy with a distinctive strawberry-like flavour. Synonyms: Red Quarrenden, Sack Apple, Scarlet Pippin.

Discovery *(d)* Mid August. Raised in about 1949 by Mr Drummer of Langham, Essex. It was first named 'Thurston August' but renamed Discovery in 1962 and introduced by nurseryman J. Matthews, Thurston, Suffolk. Fruits have firm, juicy flesh with a fairly sweet flavour and a hint of strawberry. Parentage: Worcester Pearmain x Beauty of Bath. Offspring: Limelight, Scrumptious®.

Doctor Harvey *see* Harvey.

Duke of Devonshire *(d)* Early October. Raised in 1835 by Mr Wilson, gardener to the Duke of Devonshire at Holker Hall, Lancashire. It was introduced in about 1875. Fruits have rather dry flesh with a rich, nutty flavour. Synonyms: Holker Pippin.

Dumelow's Seedling *(c/k)* Early October. Raised by Mr Dumelow (or Dumeller) at Shackerstone, Leicestershire. The original tree was growing in 1800. It was exhibited as 'Dumelow's Crab' in 1818, and renamed 'Wellington' in around 1819. Fruits have very firm, crisp, juicy flesh which is extremely acid. Cooks to a firm purée. Parentage: Northern Greening x Unknown. Offspring: Cottenham Seedling, Newton Wonder. Synonyms: Beauty, Doncklaer, Duke of Wellington, Fair Maid of Taunton, Lord Duncan, Souring, Wellington Pippin, Wellington.

Early Windsor *see* Alkmene

Easter Orange *(d)* Early October. Introduced by nurserymen, Hillier & Sons, Winchester, Hampshire. It was first recorded in 1897. Fruits have crisp flesh with a sweet and aromatic flavour.

Edith Hopwood *(d)* Early September. Raised by F. W. Thorrington, a retired London Customs Officer, Hornchurch, Essex. It was received by the National Fruit Trials in 1925. Fruits have fairly firm, crisp flesh with a slightly subacid flavour. Parentage: Cox's Orange Pippin x Unknown.

Edward VII *(c/k)* Mid October. First recorded in 1902. It was introduced by Rowe of Worcester in 1908. Fruits have fairly juicy flesh with an acid flavour which cooks to a purée. Parentage: Blenheim Orange x Golden Noble.

Egremont Russet *(d)* Late September. Thought to have originated from England. It was first recorded in 1872. Fruits have rather dry flesh with a rich, nutty flavour. It is probably the most important commercial russet in the UK at present.

Ellison's Orange *(d)* Mid September. Raised by Rev. C. C. Ellison at Bracebridge and Mr Wipf, Head Gardener to Ellison's brother-in-law at nearby Hartsholme Hall, Lincolnshire. First recorded in 1904. It was introduced by Pennells Nurseries, Lincolnshire in 1911. Fruits have soft, juicy flesh with a distinctive aniseed flavour. Parentage: Cox's Orange Pippin x Calville Blanc (Mayenne). Sports: Red Ellison's Orange.

Elton Beauty *(d)* Early September. Originated from Ince Orchards, Chester. It was introduced by 1952. Fruits have soft flesh with a moderately sharp and aromatic flavour. Parentage: James Grieve x Worcester Pearmain.

Emneth Early *(c)* Early August. Raised by William Lynn of Emneth, Norfolk. It was first recorded in 1899 and introduced by Cross of Wisbech, Cambridgeshire. Fruits are crisp, firm and very acid. Cooks to a purée. Parentage: Lord Grosvenor x Keswick Codlin. Synonyms: Early Victoria.

Epicure *(d)* Late August. Raised in 1909 by Laxton Brothers Ltd. at Bedford, England and introduced by them in 1929. Fruits have moderately firm and juicy flesh with a refreshing flavour. Parentage: Wealthy x Cox's Orange Pippin. Synonyms: Laxton's Epicure.

Estivale *see* Delbard Estivale

Fearn's Pippin *(d)* Early October. Raised in Mr Bagley's garden at Fulham, London before 1780. Fruits have firm, juicy flesh with a slightly acid and pleasant aromatic flavour. Synonyms: Clifton Nonsuch, Smiling Mary, Thomason, Waterloo.

Feltham Beauty *(d)* Mid August. Raised and introduced by Veitch & Sons Nurseries at Langley, at that time part of Buckinghamshire. First described in 1908. Fruits have firm, crisp flesh with a moderately sharp flavour. Parentage: Cox's Orange Pippin x Gladstone.

Flower of Kent *see* Isaac Newton's Tree

Fortune *(d)* Early September. Raised in 1904 by Laxton Brothers Ltd. at Bedford, England and introduced by them in 1931. Fruits have fairly firm, juicy flesh with a sweet aromatic flavour. Synonyms: Laxton's Fortune. Parentage: Cox's Orange Pippin x Wealthy. Sports: Red Fortune.

Foxwhelp *(s)* Mid September. One of the oldest surviving varieties of cider apple. It is first mentioned in John Evelyn's *Pomona* of 1664. It is thought to have originated from Gloucestershire or Herefordshire. The original cultivar is now very rare and often referred to as 'Old Foxwhelp' to distinguish it from later sports. Fruits are 'bittersharp' and contain high levels of tannin.

Fuji *(d)* Late October. Raised in 1939 by H. Niitsu at the Tohoku Horticultural Research Station, Fujisaki, Aomori, Japan. It was named in 1962. Fruits have crisp, juicy flesh with a moderately sharp flavour. Fruits often fail to mature fully in the UK. Parentage: Ralls Janet x Delicious.

Gala *(d)* Early October. Raised in about 1934 by J. H. Kidd at Greytown, Wairarapa, New Zealand. It was named in 1965. Fruits have crisp, juicy flesh with a sweet and good aromatic flavour. It is currently one of the most widely produced commercial varieties. Parentage: Kidd's Orange Red x Golden Delicious. Offspring: Kanzi®, Rubens®. Sports: Royal Gala.

Galloway Pippin *(c)* Late September. Believed to have come from Wigtown, Galloway, Scotland. It was first brought to notice in 1871 but is believed to be much older. Fruits have crisp, juicy flesh with a moderately sharp flavour. Keeps its shape when cooked.

George Cave *(d)* Early August. Raised in 1923 by George Cave at Dovercourt, Essex. It was acquired by W. Seabrook & Sons Ltd., Boreham, Essex and named in 1945. Fruits have fine-textured, juicy flesh with a slightly aromatic and pleasant flavour.

Gladstone *(d)* Late July. Thought to have originated in about 1780. It was re-discovered by Jackson, at Blakedown Nursery, Kidderminster, Worcestershire and introduced in 1868 as 'Jackson's Seedling'. It was renamed 'Mr Gladstone' in 1883. Fruits are juicy with a good aromatic flavour. Offspring: Feltham Beauty, Langley Pippin, Laxton's Early Crimson. Synonyms: Lord Gladstone, Scarlet Pippin, Striped Quarrenden.

Golden Delicious *(d/k)* Late October. A chance seedling found in 1890 by A. H. Mullins, Clay County, West Virginia, USA. It was introduced in 1914 by Stark Brothers. Fruits have crisp, sweet, juicy flesh with a good aromatic flavour. Offspring: Mutsu (Crispin), Jonagold, Gala, Greensleeves. Sports: Lemon Pippin, Starkspur® Golden Delicious.

Golden Harvey *(d/s)* Mid October. Thought to have originated in the 1600s in Herefordshire. Fruits have firm, crisp, yellow flesh with a sweet, rich, aromatic flavour. Synonyms: Brandy Apple, Guernsey Pippin.

Golden Knob *(d)* Mid October. Originated from Enmore Castle, Somerset. It has been grown since the late 1700s. Fruits have firm flesh with a sweet and nutty flavour. Synonyms: Kentish Golden Knob, Old Maid.

Golden Noble *(c)* Early October. Discovered as a chance seedling in an orchard near Downham Market by Patrick Flanagan, Head Gardener at Stow Bardolph Hall, Norfolk. It was introduced in 1820. Fruits are very juicy and acid. Cooks to a purée. Offspring: Edward VII.

Golden Pippin *(d)* Early October. Originated from England. It was recorded in 1629 by John Parkinson, Royal Botanist to Charles I. Fruits have firm, crisp flesh with a moderately sharp and rich flavour. Offspring Pitmaston Pine Apple, Court of Wick. Synonyms: Little Pippin, London Golden Pippin, Milford Pippin, Old Golden Pippin.

Golden Reinette *(d)* Early October. Thought to have originated from Europe. It has been known in England since the mid 1600s. Fruits have crisp flesh with a sweet, subacid flavour. Synonyms: Court Pendu Dore, Crackling Pippin, Elizabeth, English Pippin, Russet Pine Apple, Wicker Pippin, Wyker Pippin, Yellow German.

Granny Smith *(d)* Mid October. Discovered as a seedling growing in a compost heap in Eastwood, now in the City of Ryde, New South Wales, Australia, by Mrs Maria Ann Smith and named Granny Smith by her. Trees were known to be fruiting in 1868. Fruits have crisp, rather coarse-textured, juicy flesh with an acid flavour. Its tough skin and excellent keeping qualities made it one of the foremost supermarket varieties and one of the first to be shipped worldwide. Parentage: Thought to be a sport of French Crab.

Greensleeves (d) Mid September. Raised in 1966 by Dr Alston, East Malling Research Station, Kent. Fruits have crisp, juicy flesh with a mild, refreshing flavour. Parentage: James Grieve x Golden Delicious. Offspring: Limelight.

Grenadier (c) Mid August. First recorded in 1862 and introduced in about 1875. It was once the most widely-grown early commercial culinary apple in the UK. Fruits cook to an extremely well-flavoured, smooth purée.

Grimes Golden (d) Mid October. Raised Thomas Grimes, Brook County, West Virginia, USA. It was first known in 1804. Fruits have crisp, juicy flesh with a sweet and moderate flavour.

Hambledon Deux Ans (c/k) Early October. Originated from Hambledon, Hampshire in about 1750. Fruits have very firm, coarse-textured, rather dry flesh, which is a little sweet and slightly acid with a faint aromatic flavour. This variety is said to keep for up to two years. Synonyms: Black Blenheim, Blue Stone Pippin, Green Blenheim, Green Kitchen, Mr. Prothero, Pudding Apple, Smiling Beauty, Stone's Blenheim, Winter Hillier, Yorkshire Queen.

Harry Master's Jersey (s) Late October. Raised by Harry Masters in Yarlington, Somerset in the late 19th century. Fruits produce a medium to full bittersweet cider. Synonyms: Port Wine.

Harvey (c) Mid September. Origin unclear but believed to be named after Dr Gabriel Harvey, a former Master of Trinity College, Cambridge, who retired to Saffron Walden, Essex. It was recorded in 1629 by John Parkinson, Royal Botanist to Charles I. Fruits have firm, very dry flesh with a moderately sharp and perfumed flavour. Synonyms: Doctor Harvey, The Doctor.

Herefordshire Russet (d) Late September. Raised in 1975 by Hugh Ermen, Faversham, Kent. Introduced in 2003 by Frank P. Matthews Ltd., Tenbury Wells, Worcestershire. Fruits are crisp with a sweet, subacid flavour.

Herring's Pippin (c/d) Early September. Thought to have been raised by a Mr Herring of Lincoln. It was first recorded in 1908. Introduced by Pearson of Nottingham. Fruits have moderately firm, juicy flesh with a good aromatic almost aniseed flavour.

Hoary Morning *(c)* Early October. Thought to have been raised in Somerset. It was first recorded in 1819. The name refers to a soft, hoary bloom on the skin. Fruits have firm, dry flesh with little flavour. Synonyms: Bachelor's Glory, Dainty Apple, Downy Apple, Honeymoon, Webster's Harvest Festival.

Honey Pippin *(d)* Mid September. Raised by J. Brooke, Newmarket, Suffolk. It was received by the National Fruit Trials in 1981. Fruits are sweet, crisp and juicy with a 'honeyed' flavour.

Howgate Wonder *(c/k)* Early October. Raised in 1915–16 by George Wratten at Howgate Lane, Bembridge, Isle of Wight. It was introduced in 1932 by Stuart Low Ltd. Fruits are very large with firm, juicy, acid flesh which becomes sweeter when fully ripe. Although generally used as a culinary variety, Howgate Wonder can also be eaten fresh. Parentage: Blenheim Orange x Newton Wonder.

Isaac Newton's Tree *(c)* Mid October. Originated from a tree growing in Sir Isaac Newton's garden at Woolsthorpe Manor, near Grantham, Lincolnshire in 1660. It appears to be identical to Flower of Kent, recorded in 1629 by John Parkinson, Royal Botanist to Charles I. Fruits have soft flesh with a moderately sharp flavour.

James Grieve *(c/d)* Early September. Raised by James Grieve in Edinburgh, Scotland and introduced by his employers, Dickson's nurserymen. It was first recorded in 1893. Fruits have rather soft but very juicy flesh with a good flavour. Keeps its shape when cooked. Parentage: Pott's Seedling or Cox's Orange Pippin x Unknown. Offspring: Balder, Lord Lambourne, Greensleeves, Katja, Elton Beauty.

Jennifer Wastie *(d)* Late September. Raised by F. W. Wastie at Eynsham, Oxfordshire. It was received by the National Fruit Trials in 1945. Fruits have chewy flesh with a sweetish flavour. Parentage: Ribston Pippin x Barnack Beauty.

John Huggett *(c/d)* Late August. Raised in 1940 by John Huggett at Grange-over-Sands, at that time part of Lancashire. Fruits have fairly firm flesh with a sweet and aromatic flavour. Parentage: Allington Pippin x Unknown.

Jonagold *(d)* Mid October. Raised in 1943 at the New York State Agricultural Experiment Station, Geneva, New York. It was introduced in 1968. Fruits have juicy flesh with a sweet and rich flavour. Parentage: Golden Delicious x Jonathan.

Kanzi® *(d)* Mid September. A modern commercial dessert variety, Kanzi® is the trademark name of the 'Nicoter' cultivar developed in Belgium by

Better3fruit. *Kanzi* is Swahili for 'hidden treasure'. Introduced to the European market in around 2006. Fruits have crisp flesh with a sweet, subacid flavour. Parentage: Gala x Braeburn.

Katja *(d)* Early September. Raised in 1947 at Balsgard Fruit Breeding Institute, Sweden. It was introduced in 1966. Fruits are crisp and juicy with a pleasant flavour. Parentage: James Grieve x Worcester Pearmain. Synonyms: Katy.

Kentish Fillbasket *(c)* Mid October. Thought to have originated from Kent. It was known before 1820. Fruits have tender, acid flesh. Synonyms: Fill Basket, Kentish Pippin, Potter's Large.

Kerry Pippin *(d)* Late August. Originated from Ireland. It was first recorded in 1802. Fruits have firm, crisp but rather dry flesh with a good aromatic flavour. Synonyms: Aromatic Pippin, Donabety, Pippin Early Red, Red Streak Pippin.

Keswick Codlin *(c)* Mid August. Found growing on a heap of rubbish at Gleaston Castle near Ulverston, at that time part of Lancashire. It was recorded in 1793. Introduced by nurseryman John Sander at Keswick, Cumbria, England. Fruits have soft, somewhat dry and acid flesh.

Kidd's Orange Red *(d)* Mid October. Raised in 1924 at Greytown, Wairarapa, New Zealand by J. H. Kidd. It was introduced to the UK in about 1932. Fruits have crisp, juicy, sweet flesh with a rich aromatic flavour. Parentage: Delicious x Cox's Orange Pippin. Synonyms: Delco, Kidd's Orange. Offspring: Gala. Sports: Captain Kidd.

King Charles Pearmain *(d)* Early October. Originally received by Hogg in 1876 from nurseryman John Smith of Worcester. Fruits have firm, crisp flesh with a sweet and rich flavour.

King George V *(d)* Mid October. Raised in about 1898 by Lady Thorncroft at Bembridge, Isle of Wight. It was introduced by J. Cheal & Sons, Crawley, Sussex. Fruits have crisp, moderately juicy flesh with a subacid and good aromatic flavour. Parentage: Cox's Orange Pippin x Unknown.

King of the Pippins *(d)* Early October. The origin of King of the Pippins is confused but it appears to be identical to Reine de Reinettes grown in France. It was first recorded in 1800 and introduced by Kirke of Brompton as King of the Pippins. Its prior name appears to have been 'Golden Winter Pearmain'. Fruits are firm, juicy and moderately sharp. Synonyms include: English Winter Golden Pear, George I, George II, Jones' Southampton Pippin, Jones' Southampton Yellow, King Pippin, Orange Pearmain, Pike's Pearmain, Prince of Pippins, Princess Pippin, Queen of the Pippins, Seek-no-Further, Shropshire Pippin, Winter Gold Pearmain.

King's Acre Pippin *(d)* Mid October. First recorded in 1897. Introduced by King's Acre Nurseries, Hereford in 1899. Fruits have firm, coarse-textured, juicy flesh with a rich aromatic flavour.

Lady Hollendale *(d)* Early August. Likely to have originated from the Cambridgeshire, Lincolnshire or Norfolk Fens. It was recorded in 1918. Fruits have rather tough flesh with a sharp flavour.

Lady Sudeley *(d)* Early September. Raised in about 1849 at Petworth, Sussex. Introduced in 1885 by George Bunyard & Co., Maidstone, Kent. Fruits have firm, juicy flesh with a good flavour. Offspring: Beauty of Bedford, Benenden Early. Synonyms: Jacob's Strawberry.

Lamb Abbey Pearmain *(d)* Late September. Raised in 1804 by Mrs Mary Anne Malcolm at Lamb Abbey, Dartford, Kent. Fruits have firm, sugary and rich flesh. Parentage: Newtown Pippin x Unknown.

Lane's Prince Albert *(c/k)* Mid October. Thought to have been raised in about 1840 by Thomas Squire, Berkhamsted, Hertfordshire and named 'Albert and Victoria' after a visit by the royal couple to the area. It was renamed Lane's Prince Albert by local nurseryman John Lane and introduced by him in 1850. Fruits are very juicy and acid and cook to a purée. Parentage: Russet Nonpareil x Dumelow's Seedling. Offspring: Shoesmith, Oxford Yeoman. Synonyms: Profit, Victoria and Albert.

Laxton's Early Crimson *(d)* Early August. Raised in 1908 at Bedford, England by Laxton Brothers Ltd. and introduced by them in 1931. Fruits have rather coarse flesh with a sweet flavour. Parentage: Worcester Pearmain x Gladstone. Offspring: Merton Knave.

Laxton's Epicure *see* Epicure

Laxton's Fortune *see* Fortune

Laxton's Superb *(d)* Early October. Raised in 1897 at Bedford, England, by Laxton Brothers Ltd. and introduced by them in 1922. Fruits have firm, very juicy flesh with a sweet, pleasant and refreshing flavour. Parentage: Wyken Pippin x Cox's Orange Pippin. Offspring: Tydeman's Late Orange, Merton Pearmain. Sports: Crimson Superb.

Lemon Pippin *(c/d/k)* Early October. Thought to be English or possibly of Norman origin. Fruits have firm, dry, slightly acid flesh with a faint aromatic flavour. Synonyms: Kirke's Lemon Pippin, Pudding Apple, Quince Apple, Winter Queen.

Limelight *(d)* Mid September. Raised by Hugh Ermen, Faversham, Kent in about 1985. Introduced in 2000. Fruits have firm, juicy flesh with a fairly sweet and pleasant flavour. Parentage: Discovery x Greensleeves.

Lord Derby *(c)* Mid September. Raised by nurseryman B. W. Witham at Stockport, Cheshire. It was first recorded in 1862. Fruits are rather coarse-textured, somewhat dry with a moderately sharp flavour. It is also useful as a sharp dessert variety. Cooks to a textured purée. Parentage: Catshead x Unknown. Synonyms: Derby, London Mayor.

Lord Hindlip *(d/k)* Mid October. Raised in Worcestershire, it was first recorded in 1896 and was introduced by Watkins of Hereford. Fruits have fairly firm, juicy flesh with a good aromatic flavour. Keeps its shape when cooked. One of the longest-keeping varieties.

Lord Lambourne *(d)* Mid September. Raised in 1907 by Laxton Brothers Ltd. at Bedford, England and introduced by them in 1923. Fruits have slightly coarse-textured, juicy flesh with a sweet and good aromatic flavour. Its skin can become greasy when stored. Parentage: James Grieve x Worcester Pearmain. Siblings: Elton Beauty, Katja. Offspring: Prince Charles, Rubin. Sports: Lady Lambourne.

Lord Peckover *(d)* Mid August. It was raised at Peckover House gardens, Wisbech, Cambridgeshire and received by the National Fruit Trials in 1926. Fruits have firm, crisp flesh with a subacid flavour. Skin has a white bloom.

Lucombe's Pine *(d)* Early October. Raised in about 1800 by John Lucombe, Pince & Co. of Exeter, Devon. Fruits have tender flesh with a rich, aromatic, pineapple-like flavour. Synonyms: Lucombe's Pine Apple, Pine Apple Pippin.

Maclean's Favourite *(d)* Early October. Raised in about 1820 by Dr Allan Maclean of Sudbury, Suffolk. Fruits have a sweet and rich flavour.

McIntosh *(d)* Mid September. Discovered in 1796 by John McIntosh near Dundela, Dundas County, Ontario, Canada. Propagated by Allan McIntosh. It was introduced and named in about 1870. Fruits have rather soft, very juicy flesh with a sweet, pleasant vinous flavour. Parentage: Fameuse or Saint Lawrence x Unknown. Offspring: Tydeman's Early Worcester, Empire, Merton Charm, Jonamac, Spartan. Synonyms: MacIntosh, McIntosh Red.

Médaille d'Or *(s)* Mid November. Raised in 1865 by M. Godard of Bois-Guillaume, Normandy, France. It was introduced into England in 1884 by the Woolhope Naturalists' Field Club, Herefordshire. Fruits produce a bittersweet cider with a high alcohol content and a strong fruity flavour.

Meridian *(d)* Mid September. Raised at East Malling Research Station, Kent, by Dr Frank Alston. Introduced in 1999. Fruits have a firm, crisp texture and a Cox-like flavour. Parentage: Falstaff x Cox's Orange Pippin.

Merton Prolific *(d/k)* Mid October. Raised in 1914 by M. B. Crane at the John Innes Horticultural Institute, Merton, south-west London. It was named in 1947. Fruits have firm, crisp, tender flesh with a sweet, moderately acid flavour. Parentage: Northern Greening x Cox's Orange Pippin.

Merton Worcester *(d)* Early September. Raised in 1914 by M. B. Crane at the John Innes Horticultural Institute, Merton, south-west London. It was named in 1947. Fruits have firm, juicy flesh with a sweet pleasant flavour. Parentage: Cox's Orange Pippin x Worcester Pearmain.

Miller's Seedling *(d)* Late August. Raised in 1848 by Mr James Miller at Newbury, Berkshire. Fruits have rather soft, very juicy flesh with a sweet and refreshing flavour. Synonyms: The Shah.

Monarch *(c/k)* Early October. Raised in 1888 and introduced in 1918 by W. Seabrook & Sons Ltd., Boreham, Essex. Fruits have rather soft, somewhat coarse-textured, juicy flesh with a moderately acid flavour. Skin is slightly greasy. Parentage: Peasgood's Nonsuch x Dumelow's Seedling.

Morley's Seedling *(c)* Mid October. Raised by C. Morley, Ely, Cambridgeshire and received by the National Fruit Trials in 1928. Fruits have firm, crisp, coarse flesh with an astringent flavour. Parentage: Alfriston x Lane's Prince Albert.

Mother *(c/d)* Late September. Originated from Boston, Massachusetts, USA and first recorded in 1844. Fruits have very juicy flesh with a distinctive aromatic flavour. Synonyms: American Mother, Gardener's Apple, Queen Anne, Queen Mary. Offspring: Mrs. Phillimore.

Mrs. Phillimore *(d)* Mid October. Raised by Charles Ross and introduced by George Bunyard & Co., Maidstone, Kent. First recorded in 1896. Fruits have crisp flesh, with a sweet, fusty flavour. Parentage: Cox's Pomona x Mother. Synonyms: Miss Phillimore.

Mutsu *(c/d/k)* Mid October. Raised in Japan in 1930, it was named 'Mutsu' in 1948 but renamed 'Crispin' for the UK market in 1968. Fruits have firm, juicy flesh which is a little sweet with a refreshing and pleasant flavour. Keeps shape when cooked. Parentage: Golden Delicious x Indo. Synonyms: Crispin.

New Rock Pippin *(d/k)* Mid October. Raised in the Barnwell area of Cambridge by William Pleasance. It was first exhibited in 1821. Fruits have firm, crisp flesh with a sweet, vinous and aromatic flavour. Keeps extremely well.

Newton Wonder *(c/k)* Mid October. Raised by Taylor at King's Newton, South Derbyshire, and introduced in about 1887. Fruits have moderately juicy flesh with a subacid flavour. Cooks to a purée. Parentage: Dumelow's Seedling x Blenheim Orange. Offspring: Howgate Wonder.

Nonpareil *(d)* Mid October. Thought to be of French origin. It was introduced into England in the mid 1500s. Fruits have juicy flesh with a slightly acid and pleasant aromatic flavour. Synonyms: English Nonpareil, Golden Russet Nonpareil, Hunt's Green Nonpareil.

Norfolk Beefing *(c/k)* Mid October. Known in Norfolk since the end of the 17th century but may have originated from France or Holland. Fruits have firm, very acid flesh and tough skin. Keeps its shape when cooked. 'Beefing' (or 'Biffin') is thought to refer to the deep maroon, beef-like colour of stored fruit. 'Biffins' – Norfolk Beefing apples, slow-baked and flattened into the form of a cake – were a popular treat in Victorian times. Synonyms: Catshead Beefing, Norfolk Bearer, Norfolk Biffin, Norfolk Coleman, Winter Coleman.

Northern Greening *(c/k)* Mid October. Thought to have originated from England. First recorded in 1826. Fruits have moderately firm, a little coarse-textured, juicy flesh with an acid flavour. Synonyms: Cowarne Quoining, Kirk Langley Pippin, Langley Pippin. Offspring: Dumelow's Seedling, Merton Prolific.

Oaken Pin (of Taylor) *(d)* Late September. Originated from England, possibly the Exe Valley in Devon. It was recorded in about 1876. Fruits have tender flesh with a sweet flavour. Its name is in reference to the fruit's ellipsoid or skittle (pin) shape.

Orange Goff *(c/d)* Mid September. Thought to have originated from Kent. Recorded in 1842. Fruits have firm, crisp flesh with an acid flavour. Synonyms: Ackland Vale, Park Apple, Pork Apple, Top Apple.

Orleans Reinette *(d)* Mid October. Thought to be of French origin. It was first described in 1776. Received an Award of Merit from the Royal Horticultural Society in 1914 under the name 'Winter Ribston' and in 1921 as 'Orleans Reinette'. Fruits have firm, fine-textured flesh with a Blenheim-like flavour. Synonyms: Cardinal Pippin, Court Pendu Blanc, Crackling Pippin, Golden Reinette, New York Reinette, Winter Ribston, Wyker Pippin.

Oxford Beauty *(d)* Mid September. Raised at Eynsham, Oxfordshire by F. W. Wastie. Recorded in 1944. Fruits have crisp flesh with a sweet, subacid flavour. Parentage: Gascoyne's Scarlet x Scarlet Nonpareil.

Oxford Conquest *(d)* Mid October. Raised in 1927 at Eynsham, Oxfordshire by F. W. Wastie. Fruits have rather tough flesh with an acid flavour. Parentage: Blenheim Orange x Court Pendu Plat.

Oxford Hoard *(d)* Mid October. Raised at Eynsham, Oxfordshire by F. W. Wastie and exhibited in 1943. Fruits have coarse, tough flesh with a sweet and aromatic flavour. Parentage: Sturmer Pippin x Golden Russet.

Peasgood's Nonsuch *(c/d)* Mid September. Raised by Mrs Peasgood as a child in Grantham in about 1858 and brought with her when she moved to Stamford, Lincolnshire. It was introduced by Thomas Laxton in 1872. Fruits are moderately juicy and a little sweet. Cooks to a sweet, delicately-flavoured purée. Parentage: Catshead x Unknown. Offspring: Charles Ross, Monarch, Reverend W. Wilks, Rival.

Pig's Nose Pippin *(d)* Mid October. Thought to have originated in Hereford, England. Described in 1884 and named for its flattened crown, resembling a pig's snout. Fruits have fine, crisp flesh with a sweet flavour.

Pig's Snout *(s/c/k)* Mid October. Thought to have originated from Callington, Cornwall. Named for its unusual shape, said to resemble a pig's nose. Fruits have juicy flesh with a subacid flavour.

Pink Lady® *see* Cripps Pink

Pine Golden Pippin *(d)* Early October. Originated from the UK and first recorded in 1861. Fruits have moderately firm, juicy flesh with a fairly sweet, rich, aromatic flavour.

Pitmaston Pine Apple *(d)* Early October. Raised by Mr White, steward to Lord Foley at Witley, Worcestershire in about 1785. Introduced by Williams of Pitmaston, Worcester. Fruits are plum-sized and yellow with firm, juicy flesh and a sweet, distinctive flavour. Parentage: Golden Pippin x Unknown. Synonyms: Ananas de Pitmaston, Pineapple Pippin.

Pixie *(d)* Mid October. Raised in 1947 at the National Fruit Trials, Wisley. Fruits have crisp, fairly juicy flesh with a good aromatic flavour. Parentage: Cox's Orange Pippin or Sunset x Unknown.

Poor Man's Profit *(c)* Early October. Originated in Somerset, England and recorded in 1824. Fruits are crisp and juicy with an acid flavour.

Porter's Perfection *(s)* Late October. Originated from the orchard of Charles Porter of East Lambrook, Somerset in the 19th century and introduced in 1907. Produces a sharp juice with little astringency.

Potts' Seedling *(c)* Early September. Raised by Samuel Potts at Ashton-under-Lyne, at that time part of Lancashire, in about 1849. Fruits have rather soft, fine-textured flesh with a very sharp flavour.

Ralls Janet *(d)* Late October. Originated from the farm of Caleb Ralls in Amherst County, Virginia, USA. First known in about 1800. Fruits have crisp, tender flesh with a slightly sweet, subacid, aromatic flavour. Offspring: Fuji. Synonyms: Genet, Jefferson Pippin, Red Never Fail.

Reverend W. Wilks *(c)* Late August. Raised by Veitch & Sons Nurseries, Chelsea, London and named after the then secretary of the Royal Horticultural Society. First recorded in 1904. Fruits have crisp, juicy flesh with a moderately sharp flavour. Cooks to a purée. Parentage: Peasgood's Nonsuch x Ribston Pippin.

Ribston Pippin *(d/s)* Late September. Raised at Ribston Hall, Yorkshire from seed brought from Rouen, and planted in about 1707. Fruits have firm, moderately juicy flesh with a rich aromatic flavour. Offspring: Sturmer Pippin, Jennifer Wastie, Cox's Pomona, Cox's Orange Pippin, Reverend W. Wilks. Synonyms: Beautiful Pippin, Essex Pippin, Glory of York, Lord Raglan, Ribston Orange, Traver's Pippin.

Rosemary Russet *(d/k)* Early October. Raised in England and first described in 1831. Fruits have firm, juicy flesh with a rather acid and good flavour. Synonyms: Rosemary.

Rosy Blenheim *(d)* Early October. Raised by F. W. Thorrington, a retired London Customs Officer, Hornchurch, Essex. Received by the National Fruit Trials in 1925. Fruits have coarse flesh with a subacid, perfumed flavour. Parentage: Cox's Orange Pippin x Unknown.

Roundway Magnum Bonum *(c/d)* Early October. Raised by Mr Joy, Head Gardener at Roundway Park, Devizes, Wiltshire before 1864. Fruits have somewhat dry, coarse-textured flesh with a very sweet and distinctive pear-like flavour.

Rubens *(d)* Early October. Raised at the Horticultural Laboratory, Wageningen, The Netherlands. Recorded in 1954 and introduced in 1955. Fruits have firm, fine flesh with a sweet flavour. Parentage: Reinette Rouge Étoilee x Cox's Orange Pippin.

Rubens® *(d)* Mid October. A modern commercial apple developed by the Consorzio Italiano Vivaisti, an Italian apple growers' consortium from Ferrara, Italy. Introduced as 'Civni' in 1988 and patented in 2003, fruit of the Civni cultivar can be marketed under the Rubens® trademark if they are of sufficient quality. Fruits have a sweet and slightly aromatic flavour. Parentage: Gala x Elstar. Synonyms: Civni.

Rubinette *(d)* Late September. Raised in 1966 in Rafz, near Schaffhausen, Switzerland by plant breeder Walter Hauenstein. Fruits are crisp and juicy with a good, aromatic flavour. Grown commercially in Switzerland. Parentage: Golden Delicious x Cox's Orange Pippin.

Saint Edmund's Pippin *(d/s)* Mid September. Raised by Richard Harvey of Bury St Edmunds, Suffolk and recorded in 1875. Fruits have moderately firm, juicy flesh with good flavour. Synonyms: Early Golden Russet, St. Edmund's Russet. Offspring: Benenden Early.

Sanspareil *(d/k)* Mid October. Known in England since the late 1800s. Fruits have crisp, yellow flesh with a sweet, aromatic flavour. Keeps its shape when cooked.

Saturn *(d)* Late September. Raised at East Malling Research Station, Kent by Dr Frank Alston. First selected in 1977. Fruits are crisp and juicy with a pleasant, sweet flavour. Parentage: Starkspur® Golden Delicious x scab resistant cultivar.

Scarlet Nonpareil *(d)* Mid October. Raised in about 1773 in the garden of an inn at Esher, Surrey. Fruits have fine flesh with a moderately sharp and rich flavour. Offspring: Oxford Beauty.

Schoolmaster *(d)* Mid October. Said to have been raised from the seed of a Canadian apple in the garden of the grammar school in Stamford, Lincolnshire or in Herefordshire. Introduced in about 1880 by Thomas Laxton. Fruits have tender, coarse flesh with an acid flavour.

Scotch Bridget *(c)* Early October. Originated from Scotland. Described in 1851. Fruits have tender flesh with a moderately sharp flavour. Keeps its shape when cooked. Synonyms: White Calville.

Scotch Dumpling *(c)* Late August. Received by the National Fruit Trials in 1949 from Scotland. Fruits have fine flesh with an acid flavour. Cooks to a purée.

Slack-my-Girdle *(s)* Mid October. An old English sweet cider variety of thought to have originated from either Devon or Somerset. Synonyms: Slack-ma-Girdle, Slack-ma-Girl.

Sops-in-Wine *(c/s)* Mid September. A very old English culinary and cider apple. Fruits have red flesh, as if soaked in red wine, and a pleasant, sweet flavour.

Strawberry Pippin *(d)* Mid September. Origin unknown. Recorded in 1874. Fruits have crisp, juicy flesh with a sweet flavour.

Sturmer Pippin *(d/k)* Late October. Raised by Mr Dillistone at Rectory House, Sturmer, Essex. First recorded in 1831. Fruits have very firm, juicy flesh with a subacid, aromatic flavour. Parentage: Ribston Pippin x Nonpareil. Offspring: Ball's Pippin, King's Acre Pippin, Oxford Hoard, Merton Pippin, Merton Russet. Synonyms: Apple Royal, Creech Pearmain, Sturmer Pepping.

Sunrise *(d)* Mid September. Thought to have been raised at Welford Park, Berkshire. Recorded in 1897. Fruits have soft flesh with a sweet, subacid flavour. Parentage: Northern Spy x Unknown.

Sunset *(d)* Late September. Raised in about 1918 by G. C. Addy at Ightham, Kent and named in 1933. Fruits have firm, crisp flesh with a Cox-like flavour. Parentage: Cox's Orange Pippin x Unknown.

Suntan *(d/k)* Early October. Raised in 1955 by Dr Frank Alston at East Malling Research Station, Kent. Fruits have moderately juicy flesh with a sharp aromatic flavour. Sports: Winter Wonder®.

Sweet Lark *(c)* Mid October. Originated from West Cornwall and traditionally used for pickling.

Ten Commandments *(s/d)* Late September. Originated from Herefordshire and exhibited in 1883. Its name comes from the ten red spots visible around the core when sliced in half. Fruits have tender, red stained flesh with a sweet but acid flavour.

The Rattler *(s/d)* Early October. Originated from Penryn, Cornwall. The Rattler comes by its name because, when ripe, the seeds rattle inside the fruit when shaken. Fruits have a sharp but pleasant flavour.

Thoday's Quarrenden *(d/k)* Early October. Found in 1949 by nurseryman Ralph Thoday at Reedground Farm, Willingham, Cambridgeshire. Fruits have tender flesh with a moderately sharp flavour. It will keep until February. Parentage: Devonshire Quarrenden x Unknown.

Tom Putt *(c/s)* Early September to November. Raised in the late 1700s by Reverend Tom Putt, Rector of Trent, at that time part of Somerset. Fruits have juicy, acid flesh and produce a sharp cider. Sports: Sidney Strake. Synonyms: Coalbrook, Devonshire Nine Square, Izrod's Kernel, Jeffrey's Seedling, Marrow Bone, Ploughman.

Trajan *(d)* Late September. Raised in 1976 at East Malling Research Station, Kent. Introduced in 1989. Fruits are sweet, crisp and juicy. Synonyms: Polka.

Tremlett's Bitter *(s)* Early October. Originated from the Exe Valley, Devon. Produces a full bittersweet cider.

Tuscan *(d)* Mid September. Raised in 1976 at East Malling Research Station, Kent and introduced in 1989. Tuscan apple trees are one of a group of 'Ballerina' varieties which grow in a naturally columnar apple style with short or non-existent side branches. They are all descended from McIntosh Wijcik. Fruits are crisp and juicy. Synonyms: Ballerina Bolero, Bolero®. Parentage: Greensleeves x McIntosh Wijcik.

Tydeman's Early Worcester *(d)* Late August. Raised in 1929 by H. M. Tydeman at East Malling Research Station, Kent and introduced in 1945. Fruits have crisp, juicy flesh with a good vinous flavour. Parentage: McIntosh x Worcester Pearmain. Offspring: Folkestone. Synonyms: Early Worcester, Tydeman's Red.

Tydeman's Late Orange *(d/k)* Mid October. Raised in 1930 by H. M. Tydeman at East Malling Research Station, Kent and introduced in 1949. Fruits have very firm, crisp flesh with a rich, aromatic flavour. Parentage: Laxton's Superb x Cox's Orange Pippin.

Upton Pyne *(c/d)* Early October. Raised by nurseryman George Pyne at Topsham, Devon and named after Upton Pyne, the village from where his family originated. Introduced in 1910. Fruits have firm, juicy flesh with a somewhat acid flavour. Cooks to a purée.

Veitch's Perfection *(c/d)* Mid October. Raised and introduced by Veitch & Sons Nurseries at Exeter, Devon before 1865. Fruits have firm, coarse-textured flesh with a sweet-sharp, slightly nutty flavour.

Wayside *(d)* Late September. Raised in 1930 by Miss Cunningham of 'Wayside', Huntington Road, Cambridge. Fruits have a sweet flavour. Parentage: Charles Ross x Unknown.

William Crump *(d)* Mid October. Raised by Mr William Crump, head gardener at Madresfield Court, near Malvern, Worcestershire and exhibited by him in 1908. It was later introduced by Rowe's nursery of Worcester. Fruits have firm, juicy flesh with a sweet and rich, aromatic flavour. Parentage: Cox's Orange Pippin x Worcester Pearmain.

Winston *(d)* Mid October. Raised in 1920 by William Pope at Welford Park, Berkshire. It was introduced as 'Winter King' in 1935 and renamed Winston in 1944. Fruits have firm, juicy flesh with a sweet and aromatic flavour. Parentage: Cox's Orange Pippin x Worcester Pearmain. Synonyms: Winter King, Wintercheer.

Winter Banana *(d/s)* Early October. Raised in 1876 on the farm of David Flory near Adamsboro, Indiana, USA. Named for its alleged banana-like flavour, it was introduced in 1890. Fruits have rather soft, moderately juicy flesh with a sweet aromatic flavour.

Winter Gem *(d/k)* Early October. Raised in 1975 by Hugh Ermen at Faversham, Kent. Introduced in 1993 by Frank P. Matthews Ltd., Tenbury Wells, Worcestershire. Fruits are crisp and juicy with a rich aromatic flavour. Parentage: Cox's Orange Pippin x Grimes Golden.

Winter Wonder® *(d)* Late October. Discovered in an orchard in Braiseworth, Suffolk by Dan Neuteboom in the late 1970s and believed to be a sport of Suntan. Fruits are juicy with a moderately sharp and aromatic flavour.

Woolbrook Pippin *(d)* Mid September. Raised in 1903 by J. H. Stevens & Son, Woolbrook Nursery, Sidmouth, Devon. Fruits have firm, crisp flesh with a sweet, slightly acid, aromatic flavour. Parentage: Cox's Orange Pippin x Unknown.

Woolbrook Russet *(c)* Mid October. Raised in 1903 by J. H. Stevens & Son, Woolbrook Nursery, Sidmouth, Devon and introduced by them. Fruits have rather coarse-textured, juicy flesh with an acid flavour. Parentage: Bramley's Seedling x King's Acre Pippin.

Worcester Pearmain *(d)* Early September. Raised by Mr Hale at Swanpool, St John's, near Worcester in 1873 and introduced by Smith of Worcester in 1874. Fruits have firm, moderately juicy flesh with a sweet, pleasant, strawberry-like, flavour. Parentage: Devonshire Quarrenden x Unknown. Offspring: Discovery, Exeter Cross, Elton Beauty, Katja, Laxton's Early Crimson, Merton Worcester, Lord Lambourne, Tydeman's Early Worcester, William Crump, Winston.

Wyken Pippin *(d)* Mid October. It is thought to have been brought to the UK from seed of a continental apple from Holland in the early 1700s and raised by Lord Craven at Wyken near Coventry. Fruits have moderately firm, juicy flesh with a sweet aromatic flavour. Offspring: Laxton's Superb. Synonyms: Arley, Gerkin Pippin, German Nonpareil, Pheasant's Eye, Warwick Pippin, Warwickshire Pippin.

Yellow Ingestrie *(d)* Early September. Raised in about 1800 by Thomas Andrew Knight at Wormsley Grange, Herefordshire. Fruits have fine flesh with a rich and moderately sharp flavour. Synonyms: Early Pippin, Early Yellow, Ingestrie, Little Golden Knob, Summer Golden Pippin, White Pippin, Yellow Ingestrie Pippin. Parentage: Orange Pippin x Golden Pippin.

Yorkshire Greening *(c)* Mid October. Assumed to have originated from Yorkshire. It was first recorded in 1803. Fruits have firm, somewhat dry flesh with a very acid flavour. Synonyms: Coates' Greening, Coates's, Goose Sauce, Seek no Farther, Yorkshire Goose Sauce.

Zari® *(d)* Early September. Raised in Rillaar, Belgium in 1988 by Better3fruit. Commercial production began in 2009. Fruits have crisp, juicy flesh with a sweet to moderately sharp flavour. Parentage: Elstar x Delcorf.

Selected Varieties by Month

In the UK varieties ripen from mid-July to May. Fruits mature later in the north and seasonal fluctuations mean that every year is different. This brief guide, based on Keepers's Nursery catalogue, is intended to show some of the varieties worth looking out for at greengrocers, farmer's markets or perhaps even consider growing yourself.

	USES					SEASON OF USE (P = picking time)										
	CULINARY	DESSERT	CIDER	JUICING	KEEPER	JULY	AUGUST	SEPTEMBER	OCTOBER	NOVEMBER	DECEMBER	JANUARY	FEBRUARY	MARCH	APRIL	MAY
Adams's Pearmain		●			●				P	●	●	●	●	●		
Alfriston	●				●				P	●	●	●	●	●	●	
Allington Pippin		●			●				P	●	●					
Annie Elizabeth	●				●				P	●	●	●	●	●	●	
Arthur Turner	●							P	●	●						
Arthur W. Barnes	●							P	●							
Ashmead's Kernel		●	●	●	●				P	●	●	●	●			
Baker's Delicious		●						P								
Barnack Beauty		●			●				P	●	●	●	●	●		
Barnack Orange		●							P	●	●	●				
Beauty of Bath		●					P									
Belle de Boskoop	●	●	●						P	●	●	●	●	●	●	
Ben's Red		●						P								
Bess Pool		●			●				P	●	●	●	●	●		
Blenheim Orange	●	●						P	●	●	●					
Bloody Ploughman		●						P	●	●						
Blue Pearmain		●							P	●	●	●	●			
Bountiful	●	●			●			P	●	●						
Bramley's Seedling	●			●	●				P	●	●	●	●	●		
Brownlees' Russet		●			●				P	●	●	●	●	●		
Calville Blanc d'Hiver	●	●							P	●	●					

	USES						SEASON OF USE P = picking time									
	CULINARY	DESSERT	CIDER	JUICING	KEEPER		JULY	AUGUST	SEPTEMBER	OCTOBER	NOVEMBER	DECEMBER	JANUARY	FEBRUARY	MARCH	APRIL	MAY
Captain Kidd		●								P	●	●	●				
Catshead	●									P	●	●	●				
Charles Ross	●	●							P	●	●	●					
Chivers Delight		●								P	●	●	●				
Claygate Pearmain		●			●					P	●	●	●	●			
Coeur de Boeuf	●									P	●	●	●	●	●		
Cornish Aromatic		●								P	●	●	●				
Cornish Gilliflower		●								P	●	●	●				
Court of Wick		●							P	●	●	●					
Court Pendu Plat		●			●					P	●	●	●	●	●		
Cox's Orange Pippin		●		●	●				P	●	●	●					
Crawley Beauty	●	●								P	●	●	●	●			
D'Arcy Spice		●		●	●					P	●	●	●	●	●	●	●
Devonshire Quarrenden		●						P									
Discovery		●		●				P	●								
Dumelow's Seedling	●				●					P	●	●	●	●	●	●	
Edith Hopwood		●							P	●							
Edward VII	●				●					P	●	●	●	●	●	●	
Egremont Russet		●		●					P	●	●	●					
Ellison's Orange		●							P	●							
Elton Beauty		●							P	●	●						
Emneth Early	●							P	●								
Epicure		●						P	●								
Fortune		●							P	●							
George Cave		●						P									
Gladstone		●					P	●									
Golden Delicious		●			●					P	●	●	●	●	●	●	●
Golden Harvey		●	●	●						P	●	●	●	●	●		
Golden Noble	●									P	●	●					
Greensleeves		●	●	●					P	●							

| | USES | | | | | | SEASON OF USE | | | | | | | | | | |
	CULINARY	DESSERT	CIDER	JUICING	KEEPER		JULY	AUGUST	SEPTEMBER	OCTOBER	NOVEMBER	DECEMBER	JANUARY	FEBRUARY	MARCH	APRIL	MAY
Grenadier	•			•				P	•								
Hambledon Deux Ans	•				•					P	•	•	•	•	•		
Harvey	•								P	•	•						
Holland Pippin	•	•								P	•	•	•	•	•		
Honey Pippin		•							P	•							
Howgate Wonder	•	•		•	•					P	•	•	•	•	•		
Irish Peach		•						P									
Isaac Newton's Tree	•									P	•	•	•				
James Grieve	•	•		•					P	•							
Kentish Fillbasket	•									P	•	•	•				
Keswick Codlin	•							P	•								
Kidd's Orange Red		•								P	•	•	•				
King Charles Pearmain		•								P	•	•	•				
King of the Pippins	•	•								P	•	•					
King's Acre Pippin		•								P	•	•	•				
Lady Sudeley		•							P								
Lamb Abbey Pearmain		•								P	•	•	•				
Lane's Prince Albert	•		•	•	•					P	•	•	•	•	•		
Laxton's Early Crimson		•						P									
Laxton's Superb		•								P	•	•	•				
Lemon Pippin	•	•		•	•					P	•	•					
Lord Hindlip		•								P	•	•	•	•	•		
Lord Lambourne		•		•					P	•	•						
Maclean's Favourite		•								P	•	•					
Meridian		•								P	•	•	•	•	•		
Monarch	•				•					P	•	•	•	•			
Mother	•	•							P	•	•	•					
Mrs. Phillimore		•								P	•	•	•	•			
Mutsu (Crispin)	•	•		•	•					P	•	•	•	•	•		

P = picking time

USES / SEASON OF USE

P = picking time

	CULINARY	DESSERT	CIDER	JUICING	KEEPER	JULY	AUGUST	SEPTEMBER	OCTOBER	NOVEMBER	DECEMBER	JANUARY	FEBRUARY	MARCH	APRIL	MAY
Newton Wonder	•			•	•			P	•	•	•	•	•			
Nonpareil		•						P	•	•	•					
Norfolk Beefing	•				•			P	•	•	•	•	•	•	•	
Orange Goff	•	•					P	•	•							
Orleans Reinette		•						P	•	•	•					
Peasgood's Nonsuch	•	•					P	•	•	•						
Pitmaston Pine Apple		•						P	•	•						
Reverend W. Wilks	•						P	•								
Ribston Pippin		•	•	•				P	•	•	•	•				
Rosemary Russet		•			•			P	•	•	•	•	•			
Roundway Magnum Bonum	•	•						P	•	•	•					
Saint Edmund's Pippin		•	•	•				P	•							
Sanspareil		•			•			P	•	•	•	•	•	•	•	
Scotch Bridget	•							P	•	•						
Sturmer Pippin		•			•			P	•	•	•	•	•			
Sunset		•					P	•	•	•						
Suntan		•			•			P	•	•	•	•	•			
Tom Putt	•		•				P	•	•							
Tydeman's Early Worcester		•					P	•								
Tydeman's Late Orange		•		•	•			P	•	•	•	•	•	•		
Upton Pyne	•	•						P	•	•	•	•	•			
William Crump		•						P	•	•	•	•	•			
Winter Banana		•	•	•				P	•	•	•	•				
Winter Gem		•			•			P	•	•	•	•	•			
Worcester Pearmain		•		•			P	•	•							
Wyken Pippin		•						P	•	•	•	•				
Yorkshire Greening	•							P	•	•	•	•	•	•		

BIBLIOGRAPHY

Adam's Apples, www.adamapples.blogspot.co.uk

Bon Appétit, www.bonappetit.com

'Breadfruit', *Devon Apples*. devon-apples.co.uk. Online at http://devon-apples.co.uk/
directory/9/Breadfruit/ (accessed 10 April 2018).

Brogdale Collections, www.brogdalecollections.org

Browning, Frank, *Apples: The Story of the Fruit of Temptation* (New ed.), Penguin
Books Ltd, 2000

Buchan, Ursula, 'The hunt for Peasgood's Nonsuch' in *The Telegraph* dated 16 October
2004. Online at https://www.telegraph.co.uk/gardening/3324079/The-hunt-for-
Peasgoods-Nonsuch.html (accessed 9 April 2018).

'Chisel Jersey', *Wikipedia*. Wikipedia.org, 17 September 2016. Online at
https://en.wikipedia.org/wiki/Chisel_Jersey (accessed 9 March 2018).

Clark, Michael, *Apples: A Field Guide*, Tewin Orchard, 2015

Clifford, Sue, and King, Angela, *The Apple Sourcebook*, Hodder & Stoughton, 2007

Colnbrook.info. 'This Apple Fair, rediscover the secrets of 1835 at The Lawns,
Bath Road'. Online at http://www.colnbrook.info/this-apple-fair-rediscovering-
the-secrets-of-1835-at-the-lawns-bath-road/ (accessed 21 March 2018).

Common Ground, www.commonground.org.uk

Copas, Liz, 'Dorset Sweet and Sour', *Dorset Life*. DorsetLife.co.uk, April 2011.
Online at http://www.dorsetlife.co.uk/2011/04/dorset-sweet-and-sour/
(accessed 30 May 2018).

'Cornish Gilliflower', *Wikipedia*. Wikipedia.org, 24 February 2016. Online at
https://en.wikipedia.org/wiki/Cornish_Gilliflower (accessed 9 March 2018).

Diacono, Mark, 'Growing apples: a gardener's guide' in *The Telegraph* dated
12 October 2015. Online at https://www.telegraph.co.uk/gardening/grow-to-eat/
growing-apples--a-gardener-s-guide (accessed 20 May 2018).

Don, Monty, 'Apple of his eye' in *The Guardian* dated 29 October 2000. Online at
https://www.theguardian.com/lifeandstyle/2000/oct/29/gardens (accessed
9 April 2018).

Don, Monty, 'Mistletoe and vine' in *The Guardian* dated 16 December 2001. Online
at https://www.theguardian.com/lifeandstyle/2001/dec/16/gardens (accessed
9 April 2018).

East of England Apples and Orchards Project, 'Bedfordshire apple varieties'.
Online at http://www.applesandorchards.org.uk/images/020_Bedfordshire_
apples.pdf (accessed 27 March 2018).

East of England Apples and Orchards Project, 'Cambridgeshire apple varieties'.
Online at http://www.applesandorchards.org.uk/images/030_Cambridgeshire_
apples.pdf (accessed 27 March 2018).

East of England Apples and Orchards Project, 'Essex apple varieties'. Online at
http://www.applesandorchards.org.uk/images/040_Essex_apples.pdf (accessed
27 March 2018).

East of England Apples and Orchards Project, 'Hertfordshire apple varieties'. Online at http://www.applesandorchards.org.uk/images/050_Hertfordshire_apples.pdf (accessed 27 March 2018).

East of England Apples and Orchards Project, 'Lincolnshire apple and pear varieties'. Online at http://www.applesandorchards.org.uk/images/060_Lincolshire_apples_and_pears.pdf (accessed 27 March 2018).

East of England Apples and Orchards Project, 'Norfolk apple varieties'. Online at http://www.applesandorchards.org.uk/images/070_Norfolk_Apples.pdf (accessed 27 March 2018).

East of England Apples and Orchards Project, 'Suffolk apple and pear varieties'. Online at http://www.applesandorchards.org.uk/images/080_Suffolk_Apples_and_Pears.pdf (accessed 27 March 2018).

Eat the Seasons, www.eattheseasons.co.uk

el Restaurante, 'Apples and Pears: Harvesting Fruit on Mexican Menus'. Online at http://elrestaurante.com/apples-and-pears-harvesting-fruit-on-mexican-menus/ (accessed 9 April 2018).

England in Particular, 'Orchards, Trees & Orchard Produce. Some Hampshire Fruit'. Online at http://www.englandinparticular.info/orchards/o-hants-f.html (accessed 21 March 2018).

English Apples & Pears, www.englishapplesandpears.co.uk

EOL, Encyclopedia of Life, 'Orchard Apple – Malus domestica'. Online at http://eol.org/pages/629094/overview (accessed 27 March 2018).

Friends of the Tarte Tatin. 'History of the Tarte Tatin'. Online at http://www.tartetatin.org/home/history-of-the-tarte-tatin (accessed 13 May 2018).

FruitFinder, People's Trust for Endangered Species. Online at https://ptes.org/campaigns/traditional-orchard-project/fruitfinder

Fruit ID, http://www.fruitid.com

Garden Apple I.D., www.gardenappleid.co.uk

Gloucestershire Orchard Trust. 'Gloucestershire Apples Listing'. Online at https://glosorchards.org/home/fruitvarieties/gloucestershire-apples-listing (accessed 4 April).

Greenoak, Francesca, *Forgotten Fruits: the English Orchard and Fruit Garden*, Andre Deutsch, 1983

Hargreaves, Clare, 'Regional food: Shropshire fidget pie', *BBC Countryfile Magazine*, 10 March 2011. Online at http://www.countryfile.com/countryside/regional-food-shropshire-fidget-pie (accessed 6 October 2017).

Hogg, Dr Robert, and Graves Bull, Dr Henry, *The Herefordshire Pomona – facsimile*, Woolhope Naturalists Field Club, 1885, Wheeler, Richard (Ed.) CD ROM, The Marcher Apple Network, 2005

Home Orchard Society, www.homeorchardsociety.org

'Howgate Wonder'. *Brogdale Collections*, 'The National Fruit Collection – Howgate Wonder', 4 October 2017. http://www.brogdalecollections.org/apples-national-fruit-collection-howgate-wonder/ (accessed 10 April 2018).

Hursh Graber, Karen, 'September in the Mexican sierra: an abundance of apples', MexConnect. Online at http://www.mexconnect.com/articles/3515-september-in-the-mexican-sierra-an-abundance-of-apples (accessed 9 April 2018).

Leighton, Christine, 'History of Ashmead's Kernel', 31 December 2009. Gloucestershire Orchard Group. Archived June 7, 2011 at the Wayback

Machine. Online at https://web.archive.org/web/20110607212742/
http://www.gloucestershireorchardgroup.org.uk/varieties/apples/ashmeads-
kernel-history/ (accessed 21 March 2018).

Love British Food, www.lovebritishfood.co.uk

Mann, Gertrude, *Apple Book: Recipe for Every Month of the Year*, Millington Books, 1981

Marcher Apple Network, www.marcherapple.net

Martin, Alice A., *All About Apples* (First ed.), Houghton Mifflin, Boston, 1976

Monbiot, George, 'Fallen fruit' in *The Guardian* dated 30 October 2004. Online at
https://www.theguardian.com/lifeandstyle/2004/oct/30/foodanddrink.weekend
(accessed 4 July 2018).

Morgan, Joan, and Richards, Alison, *The New Book of Apples* (Rev. ed.), Ebury Press, 2002

Morris, D. and Wilks, Rev. W, ed., *British Apples*, Report of the Apple and Pear
Conference, 1888, *Journal of the Royal Horticultural Society*, vol. X, 1888; published
as a separate volume.

National Fruit Collection, University of Reading and Brogdale Collections,
www.nationalfruitcollection.org.uk

'Norfolk Beefing', *Wikipedia*. Wikipedia.org, 15 March 2017. Online at
https://en.m.wikipedia.org/wiki/Norfolk_Biffin (accessed 9 April 2018).

Oram, Steve, 'DNA Dissection' in People's Trust for Endangered Species (PTES)
Winter Newsletter, January 2018.

Orange Pippin, www.orangepippin.com

'Ozark Pudding', Wikipedia. Wikipedia.org, 3 April 2018. Online at
https://en.m.wikipedia.org/wiki/Ozark_pudding (accessed 25 April 2018).

'Pippin Pie – an English Heritage Recipe for Audley End Apple Festival',
Sneaky-Veg. SneakyVeg.com, 23 September 2015. Online at
https://www.sneakyveg.com/pippin-pie-an-english-heritage-recipe-for-audley-
end-apple-festival (accessed 29 May 2018).

'Pippin Pie', *The Foods of England Project*. foodsofengland.co.uk, 20 January 2018.
Online at http://www.foodsofengland.co.uk/pippinpie.htm (accessed 29 May 2018).

Poiteau, Pierre Antoine, *Pomologie Française: Recueil Des Plus Beaux Fruits Cultivés
En France – facsimile*, (vol. 4), 1846

Pollan, Michael, *The Botany of Desire* (New ed.), Bloomsbury Publishing Plc,
New York, 2003

Popescu, Charlotte, *The Apple Cookbook*, Cavalier Paperbacks, 1997

Postcards from Slough. 'Cox's Orange Pippin'. Online at http://www.postcards-
from-slough.co.uk/home/cox-s-orange-pippin (accessed 21 March 2018).

Quinton, A. R. (Illustrator), and Salmon, J. (Compiler), *Favourite Apple Recipes*,
J Salmon, 2002

Roach, F. A., *Cultivated Fruits of Britain: Their Origin and History*, Basil Blackwell, 1985

'Roman Britain', *Wikipedia*. Wikipedia.org, 23 April 2018. Online at
https://en.wikipedia.org/wiki/Roman_Britain (accessed 25 April 2018).

Rowson, Geoffrey, 'Christmas Pippin – a winner?' Fruit Forum. Online at
http://www.fruitforum.net/christmas-pippin-a-winner-.htm (accessed
4 April 2018).

Sainsbury, Jill, 'Uncovering an orchard', BBC Dorset, Nature Features, 10 October
2008. Online at http://www.bbc.co.uk/dorset/content/articles/2008/10/10/
orchard_feature.shtml (accessed 30 May 2018).

Sanders, Rosanne, *The English Apple*, Phaidon Press, First Edition, 1988

Shields, Steffie, 'Apples in abundance' in *Lincolnshire Life* dated October 2015.
Online at http://www.lincolnshirelife.co.uk/posts/view/apples-in-abundance
(accessed 18 September 2018).

'Silk Road', *Wikipedia*. Wikipedia.org, 25 April 2018. Online at
https://en.wikipedia.org/wiki/Silk_Road (accessed 25 April 2018).

Silverman, Laura, 'Why we are eating the wrong kind of apples' in *The Telegraph*
dated 18 October 2014. Online at https://www.telegraph.co.uk/foodanddrink/
healthyeating/11171530/Why-we-are-eating-the-wrong-kind-of-apples.html
(accessed 10 October 2017).

Slough History Online. 'Green Fields of Slough. An Apple a Day'. Online at
http://www.sloughhistoryonline.org.uk/ixbin/hixclient.exe?a=query&p=
slough&f=generic_theme.htm&_IXFIRST_=1&_IXMAXHITS_=1&%3Dtheme_
record_id=sl-sl-coxorange (accessed 21 March 2018).

Smith, Muriel W. G, *National Apple Register of the United Kindgom*, Ministry of
Agriculture, Fisheries and Food, 1971.

Spencer, Richard, 'Struggle to save the apple's Asian birthplace' in *The Telegraph*
dated 21 August 2009. Online at https://www.telegraph.co.uk/news/worldnews/
asia/kazakhstan/6068161/Struggle-to-save-the-apples-Asian-birthplace.html
(accessed 1 July 2018).

'Squab pie', *Wikipedia*. Wikipedia.org, 2 April 2018. Online at
https://en.wikipedia.org/wiki/Squab_pie (accessed 23 April 2018).

'Tarte Tatin', *Wikipedia*. Wikipedia.org, 1 March 2018. Online at
https://en.wikipedia.org/wiki/Tarte_Tatin (accessed 13 May 2018).

Taylor, H. V., *The Apples of England*, (3rd ed.), Crosby Lockwood & Son, 1945

'Teynham History: Richard Harrys, Henry VIII's Fruiterer, and Cherries',
Teynham Parish Council Website. Online at http://teynham.org/richard_
harrys.html (accessed 2 July 2018).

The Big Apple Association, www.bigapple.org.uk

The English Apple Man, www.theenglishappleman.com

The Foods of England Project, www.foodsofengland.co.uk

The Kitchn, www.thekitchn.com

'The Last Wild Apple Forests', *Atlas Obscura*. Atlasobscura.org. Online at
https://www.atlasobscura.com/places/the-last-wild-apple-forests (accessed
1 July 2018).

Tingle, Rory, 'The British apple is under threat' in *The Independent* dated 21 October
2014. Online at https://www.independent.co.uk/life-style/food-and-drink/
features/the-british-apple-is-under-threat-9807665.html (accessed 4 July 2018).

UK Food in Season, www.carta.co.uk/beebstuff/seasons

Vegetarian Society, www.vegsoc.org

Vidal, John, 'British apple boom brings back hundreds of forgotten varieties' in
The Guardian dated 21 October 2017. Online at https://www.theguardian.com/
lifeandstyle/2017/oct/21/british-apple-boom-forgotten-varieties-apple-day
(accessed 10 April 2018).

'Waldorf salad', *Wikipedia*. Wikipedia.org, 29 April 2018. Online at
https://en.wikipedia.org/wiki/Waldorf_salad (accessed 2 June 2018).

Wheeler, Richard (Ed.), *Vintage Fruit – Cider Apples and Perry Pears – facsimile*,
CD ROM, The Marcher Apple Network, 2007

Woodier, Olwen, *The Apple Cookbook*, Storey Books, 2015

ᴀCKNOWLEDGEMENTS

I would like to thank every person who helped *Little Gem Apple* become a reality.

First and foremost my husband, Geoff: for his encouragement and support every step of the way; for tasting every recipe, accompanying me to every orchard and Apple Day event; and for coming up with the subtitle. My dad, whose Howgate Wonder provided the inspiration for this book. Jeannine Dillon, David Hearn and Helen Brown for all their help and advice. And, Helena Caldon for kindly editing the recipes.

I am grateful to Marcher Apple Network for permission to reproduce images from *The Herefordshire Pomona – facsimile* CD ROM on the cover.

Keepers Nursery for permission to use information from their website on the list of selected varieties by month on pages 184–187.

Steve Oram, Orchard Biodiversity Officer at People's Trust for Endangered Species and Dr Matthew Ordidge of School of Agriculture, Policy and Development at the University of Reading for their assistance.

Good apples all.